PARENTAL GUIDANCE SERIES

THE BEAUTY OF VIRGINITY
TIMELY MORAL INSTRUCTIONS FOR BOYS AND GIRLS
(WITH QUESTIONS AND ANSWERS)

REMI OLUYALE

Unless otherwise indicated, all scripture quotations in this book are from the King James Version (KJV) of the Bible.

THE BEAUTY OF VIRGINITY
Copyright © 2006 Remi Oluyale
Second Edition 2016
ISBN: 978-37718-9-2

Printed by CreateSpace

<u>DEDICATION</u>

This book is dedicated to our children: **Tayo**, **David**, **Favour** and **Praise**. You are wonderful kids, bundles of joy and anointed for your generation. Special love from **Daddy** and **Mummy**.

CONTENT

Introduction

Welcome to the Parental Guidance Series. Parents have a responsibility over their children to train and bring them up in the way they should go. *"Train up a child in the way he should go and when he is old, he will not depart from it" (Prov. 22: 6)*. There is a way every child should go and a way a child should not go. Every child needs to be brought up in the way he should go. This presupposes that parents and guardians should have an idea of the way a child should go. Parents have a responsibly to train up their children to follow the ways of the lord, respect constituted authorities and learn how to obey instructions.

The Beauty Of Virginity

A child has the way he should go. There is a way a child should go in reference to vocation and morality. It is the responsibility of parents to help each child discover his/her abilities and follow that direction in life. The only place of true fulfilment in life is in discovering and fulfilling divine purpose. Parents are also required to help a child set a good moral foundation that the child can build on later in life. Children usually don't know where they should go. They are new to this world. The responsibility of guidance is therefore on the parents. When children are not given a sense of direction by their parents or guardians, they are ready to go anywhere or try anything.

In this book, we are considering what virginity is, God's purpose for virginity and how parents can guide their children in the will of God concerning virginity. The rate of moral laxity and premarital sexual consciousness among the youths calls for a reorientation from the parents to guide their children to be morally and sexually upright. When children are not given the right information about sex and sexuality, they readily pick up junks and perversions from friends, magazines, internet, television, novels, films etc. Since children are naturally adventurous, they will surely practise whatever information they have.

Introduction

Most parents don't know what to say to their children about sex because they were also not told anything by their own parents. They had to discover many things for themselves after making several mistakes. This book is to assist parents to know what to tell their children about sexuality. Parents should also allow their teenagers to read this book and discuss the issues raised with them. The purpose of this book is not to condemn those who married as non-virgins or young people who had lost their virginity. The purpose rather is to encourage the unmarried to be chaste, desist from further premarital sex and to equip those who haven't lost their virginity to know why and how they should keep it. It is also for parents to know how to guide their children.

1
What is Virginity?

Virginity is a state of being sexually pure, untouched and undefiled. A virgin is a male or a female who has never had sexual intercourse. There is no significant sign to determine a male virgin. In females, the presence of the hymen is a sign of virginity. The hymen is a membrane that partially covers the entrance to the vagina. The hymen is usually physically torn and bleeds when a woman engages in her first sexual intercourse. The bloodstained bed-sheet is the proof of a woman's purity and this is significantly celebrated in many cultures and religions.

The Beauty Of Virginity

Quoting from Wikipedia, a free encyclopaedia on the internet: "The presence of an intact membrane is often seen as physical evidence of virginity in the broader technical sense. The absence of one, however, is not necessarily an indication of participation in sexual intercourse, since in some women the hymen is either absent from birth, or sufficiently vestigial *not to be affected by sexual penetration.* Also, the hymen can be broken before a woman engages in sexual intercourse, for example during strenuous exercise or during the insertion of a tampon. Conversely, in rare cases a woman's hymen is imperforate, and as menstrual discharge cannot then escape, surgical intervention to break it is necessary to protect her health"[1].

In many cultures and traditions, virginity is of a prime importance in marriage ceremonies. In some cultures, virginity testing is very common. Among the Bantu of South Africa, virginity testing typically involves a female elder carrying out a personal inspection on the bride.

The virginity of a bride is a serious matter in many cultures. "In many Mediterranean and African cultures, the husband's family may take revenge through violent punishments and banishment of the bride because the "non-virgin" bride "shamed" them. Among the Yungar people of Australia,

What Is Virginity?

girls without the hymen before marriage were starved, tortured, or even killed. In Arab countries, the "non-virgin" brides may be killed by her brothers, uncles, or even fathers. The perpetrators often escape prosecution due to the strong customs that justify such murders"[2]

In ancient Athens, the law required that young women who lost their virginities before marriage be sold into slavery, because that was all they were worth once they had ruined their reputations and their family honour. Roman law allowed fathers to murder their daughters and the men who had seduced them if the daughters lost their virginities before marriage.[3]

Among the Yoruba people of south-west Nigeria, an empty matchbox is presented to the bride's mother if the bride was not '*found at home*" that is, a non-virgin. This is usually a thing of shame for the bride's family. The bride is considered to be of a less value and may be treated as such by her in-laws. If however, the bride was "*found at home*" that is a virgin, a match box tucked with the bloodstained cotton-wool is presented to the bride's mother with a lot of appreciation to the mother for keeping her daughter pure. This is often celebrated and the symbol is well kept by the mother. This practice is however gradually eroding away as a result of modernization and infiltration of western cultures.

Traditionally in western marriage ceremonies, a veil is taken as a symbol of the bride's virginity. However, as a result of 'modernism' and permissiveness in western culture, premarital virginity is no longer regarded as a virtue. Youths are even encouraged to experience sexual intercourse for as long as it appeals to them. They are only advised to use protective means like the condom. This development has highly encouraged and promoted promiscuity to the extent that it is almost becoming out of fashion to remain a virgin as a teenager! This high level of promiscuity and condolence of multiple sexual partners among the unmarried is the bedrock of immorality and sexual unfaithfulness which often leads to separation and/or divorce later in marriage. In the olden days when sexual purity was upheld, the rate of divorce was very low as compared to what we have to cope with today.

In the Bible, the Old Testament Hebrew word "Almah" was translated: 'Virgin', 'damsel', 'maid' and 'lass'. A bride was expected to be a virgin. If a man rapes a virgin, then he must marry her without the option of divorcing her later on. If the father refused to give her daughter to such a man, the rapists was made to pay heavily (50 shekels of silver) for defiling a virgin (Exo. 22:16-17, Deut. 22:28-29). The man was made to pay heavily for defiling a virgin because once disvirgined, no other man will pay so much on her again.

If a man marries a woman and finds her to be a non-virgin in truth after marrying her, she shall be put to death. *"...... But if this thing be true, and the tokens of her virginity be not found for the damsel: Then they shall bring out the damsel to the door of her father's house, and the men of her city shall stone her with stones that she die because she hath wrought folly in Israel, to play the whore in her father's house: so shall thou put evil away from among you" (Deut 22:13-21).* In the laws given to Moses for Israel, God awarded capital punishment for brides who were discovered to be non-virgins to show how serious the offence is from God's point of view. Premarital sex is evil according to the above scriptures and I believe God still stands by His words. God's words remain the same.

The high priests strictly married virgins according to the divine commandment *"And he shall take a wife in her virginity...." (Lev. 21:13-15)* To do otherwise was profanity of the anointing and the lord's sanctification over him.

When Jesus Christ was to be born, only a virgin qualified to be the mother of the messiah. Isaiah the prophet gave the prophecy of a virgin birth several years earlier and the prophecy was fulfilled in Virgin Mary.

The believers are also referred to as the virgin brides of Christ. Sin is what defiles the spiritual virgins of Christ. Paul in his second letter to the Corinthians wrote: *"for I am jealous over you with godly jealousy: for I have espoused you to one husband, that I may present you as a chaste virgin to Christ" (II Cor. 11:2).* This is why all believers in spite of their physical virginity status are referred to as virgins of Christ. This is a spiritual virginity and does not mean anything physical. A non-virgin (physically) therefore does not become a physical virgin as a result of salvation in Christ. This is because salvation (a spiritual event), does not replace the broken hymen. However, there can be a secondary "virginity" which means that a person, who had lost his /her virginity before salvation, decides to maintain a state of sexual purity afterwards. To still indulge in premarital sex after salvation is a loss of this secondary "virginity". Primary virginity therefore means

What Is Virginity?

never to have been indulged in sexual intercourse either before or after salvation (as a Christian).

Virginity is a sign of purity and chastity. The issue of virginity is mostly directed at women but the men are also required by God to be virgins until marriage. The divine instructions pertaining to morality and sexual purity are not solely directed to women. The commandments are meant for both men and women to keep. A man who has never had sex for once is also a virgin even thought there is nothing physically to show as a proof for it.

Virginity is still highly regarded in some cultures that women are faking it with a minor surgical operation called 'hymenorrhaphy'. Hymenorrhaphy is a surgical repair of the broken hymen. Pieces of the hymen are sown back with a gelatin capsule containing a blood like substance which breaks and makes it look like blood during the faked 'first' sexual experience. Hymenorrhaphy costs between US$100-600 in Egypt. In Turkey, It goes for between US$140-1500[4]. Marriage should not be based on deceit but love, respect and decency.

2
Created For A Purpose

God is a God of purpose. Everything God created was created for a specific purpose. Every organ in the body is important as every part of the body was created by God to meet a purpose.

The purpose of the sex organs in the human body is for the purpose of pleasure and procreation. Without the sex organs, humans would not be able to reproduce, multiply and fill the earth. Biologically, the function of the human hymen is still uncertain but scientists hypothesize that it protects the vagina from infection in infants.

The Beauty Of Virginity

God instituted the marriage institution for families to be raised. In the original plan of God for marriage, a virgin man is to be married to a virgin woman. Adam and Eve were virgins. They came together as husband and wife to raise the first family on earth. God designed sex to function effectively only within marriage. Premarital sex was not in the plan and purpose of God for man. Sex within marriage is godly, holy and good. Outside marriage, sex is ungodly, sinful and bad. It is also destructive and regrettable outside the confine of marriage as designed by God, the creator.

God purposed virginity to be kept till the wedding night but after man fell, sin came and turned the whole arrangement upside down. Man became rebellious and disobedient to divine laws and instructions so much that premarital sex, fornication, adultery and all forms of sexual perversion became the order of the day.

Man degenerated morally to the extent that at a time, God had to wipe out the whole world with water except the household of Noah. There was another time God had to destroy Sodom and Gomorrah with fire and brimstone falling from heaven because of their moral laxity and sexual perversion. The men of Sodom and Gomorrah were so sexually perverted that they asked Lot to bring out the men (angels) who came to visit him for them to have sex with them. This sounds like the gay activists of today! Apart from Lot and his household, not one single soul escaped the destruction that came on Sodom and Gomorrah. God is not less displeased today than He was on Sodom and Gomorrah. God is patient with man to see how many will turn from wickedness and embrace salvation in Christ because God already sent his son to offer himself as a sacrifice for the sin of mankind. For those who will refuse salvation and follow their own ways, eternal fire and damnation is already being prepared for them.

The golden gift

Virginity is a special gift a woman keeps for her husband till the wedding night. The man also keeps himself as a special gift for his bride by being chaste. Men naturally wish to marry virgins. Men are possessive and always wish no other man ever shared their wives. Even those men that had disvirgined many women still hope that the woman they would marry should be a virgin. Virginity means 'special' 'clean' and 'preserved'. Today, people talk about virginity disparagingly because of their lack of morality and godliness.

Disvirgined boys and girls will talk down on a peer that is preserved in a way to make the virgin feel out of place and join the bandwagon. They do this because they feel condemned by the presence of a pal like them who is able to hold his/her head high in the midst of corruption that has engulfed them. The bible says Noah condemned his generation by his act of righteousness (Heb. 11:7). Everybody else in Noah's day was wicked except Noah. It was like nobody could be righteous, but Noah proved them wrong by his righteousness. It then follows that it was possible for anybody to be righteous like Noah if only they chose to. All the wicked people were wicked because they chose to be wicked. (If you are a virgin and your friends are laughing and mocking you, it's because they are feeling condemned and wish you become like them since it's too late for them to remain like you. They are actually envying you. Don't be deceived to join them. You are special! Keep your golden gift for your future spouse).

The spiritual purpose
Virginity has a very deep spiritual significance. That is why divine laws in the Old Testament concerning virginity were very strict and defaulters were stoned to death.

Created For A Purpose

The marriage union is a covenant which signifies oneness. Husband and wife become spiritually joined together. A real covenant must involve blood, sometimes the blood of animals or the blood of the partners in that covenant. In God's arrangement, the marriage covenant is to be sealed with a mixing of blood from the husband and wife during their very first sexual intercourse on the wedding night. The hymen in the woman ruptures and bleeds as the man penetrates into the woman. The man also ejaculates and the semen is mixed with the flowing blood from the hymen, staining the bed-sheet. This mixing of blood and semen is the actual cutting of the marriage covenant. This act could be painful to the woman, but it registers something like 'special' and 'tender' in the heart of the man towards the woman. If men will do things right, things will go right.

The spiritual significance of what takes place from the joining during the wedding ceremony and is consummated on the wedding night cannot be quantified with words. Paul called it a great mystery:

"For this cause shall a man leave his father and mother, and shall be joined unto his wife and they two shall be

one flesh. This is a great mystery: but I speak concerning Christ and the church".   (Eph. 5:31-32)

Sex in itself possesses a deep spiritual significance. Sex is not just having fun. It is both a physical and spiritual affair. When husband and wife marry as virgins, they fulfil the perfect picture of the mystery of oneness as ordained by God. Their spirits are perfectly joined to each other without any fragmentation. On the other hand, when one or both partners already had other sexual partners before coming together, their spirits cannot perfectly align as husband and wife because parts of them are in their previous sex partners and vice versa. This is what I call 'spiritual fragmentation'. This thing is very real and true because the scriptures cannot be broken:

"What? Know ye not that he which is joined to an harlot is one body? For two, saith he, shall be one flesh"
(I Cor. 6:16)

The spiritual is very dynamic. A man or a woman can be joined to several previous sex partners and his spouse at the same time. Of course, this is not a perfect spiritual joining because a man should be joined to only one woman and a woman should be joined to only one man to achieve that perfect oneness.

Little wonder a woman never forgets about her previous sex partners especially, the guy who broke her virginity, who definitely has a special place in her spirit. She may not have a heart for them as she is trying to focus her heart and mind energy on her husband, but they are still there in her spirit. Somehow, she feels and knows there is still a link until such connections are broken in the name of Jesus during a deliverance session. The same thing goes for the man. The power in the name of Jesus alone is what can severe these unholy and ungodly contacts for the spiritual power of those fragmentations to be broken. Confess to your spouse, receive forgiveness, mention the names of those previous sex partners one by one and break every covenant cut with them through sex in the name of Jesus. This is the only way out. Otherwise, your marriage will suffer the grave consequences whether you are aware of the facts or not! The best way is still God's way i.e. preservation of virginity until marriage.

3
The Lures Of The Serpent

Thethiefcomethnot,butfortosteal,and to kill, and to destroy: I am come that they might have life, and that they might have it more abundantly".

(John 10:10)

The devil is a thief. Most girls that were disvirgined before marriage usually attest to it that they felt the man who disvirgined them stole something from them. The main ministry of the devil is to steal, to kill and to destroy.

The serpent (devil) is behind all forms of sexual immorality like premarital sex (fornication), adultery and sexual pervasions like homosexuality, lesbianism, anal sex etc.

The Beauty Of Virginity

Satan intends to steal a man/woman's virginity through premarital sex, kill love in marriage and destroy the home. Satan hates the family institution with a great passion. He laughs when husband and wife deceive themselves, fight and go their different ways.

Satan is the one luring the younger generation into moral laxity and the so called "sexual revolution'. The main aim of the devil is to destroy the home. He is aware of how devastating an effect that moral laxity can have on the family and the society. Some of the avenues the serpent is using vehemently to lure this generation into sexual permissiveness and disregard for moral values like the sacredness of virginity are:

1. Television:
The TV, like any other tool/invention can be used positively or negatively. It depends on the kind of people in charge. The real purpose of the media is for information, enlightenment and entertainment. These are positive virtues and purposes if only we can have the right people legislating and running the media.

The Lures Of The Serpent

The television ranks as number one on the list of tools being adopted by Satan to lure young people into premarital sex. The television combines the powers of sight and sound, appealing to the mind through both eyes and ears. Even when a child is not yet conscious of his/her sexuality, the TV wakes up that area in the child through different kinds of obscenity on the screen. When a child watches a boy and a girl having sex right on the screen, he/she starts wondering what is happening. If there is nobody around to explain to the child, he/she may try to find out through experimentation.

Parents should moderate the programs they allow their children to watch on the TV or listen to on the radio. Each family has the right to prevent or stop evil to be broadcast into their homes by being selective with the stations and programs they watch or listen to. The problem is usually that parents no longer have the time for their children. Daddy and mummy both spend all the time with their jobs and leave the children to be tutored by the television and housemaids or house-boys. There is no way parents can properly monitor their children without investing that golden commodity called: **TIME!**

The Beauty Of Virginity

There is no way the TV can be exonerated from the moral decadence being witnessed in this generation. Most of the films shown on the television channels present regular and consistent doses of violence, foul language, illicit sex and drug abuse. By the time a youth had been feeding regularly on TV programs and films with sexual themes, he/she feels premarital sex is normal since 'everybody' is doing it. The 'everybody' in this case are the actors/actresses on the screen!

If a TV station is airing morally poisonous programs, those programs should not be watched. Parents should enlighten their children to be able to discern good and bad television programs on their own. When bad programs or films are being aired, children should be instructed to always switch off from that station.

Children should not be allowed to spend too much time watching television. If children are left alone to themselves, they can hurt themselves. It is part of parental guidance to moderate children's exposure to television.

2. **Modern music**:
Music is another powerful medium that affects the behaviour of its listeners. The lyrics of a musical piece are driven far

The Lures Of The Serpent

into the mind of the listeners by the melody of the music. The chorus of the song is repeated over and over to lay emphasis and create melody. Music is powerful. It's easier to memorize whatever is turned into a song!

Music in the olden days was composed with high moral standards. Today, because morality has fallen considerably in the society, different kinds of unthinkable words are being put into music and fed to the unsuspecting public. There are different kinds of music like: hip-hop, metals, rock etc. that are targeted at youths. Most of such music promotes immorality because of the beat and the lewd lyrics that usually make such music a sold-out!

Most of the rock artists indulge in drugs and illicit sex. In fact, most of the modern day music vividly describes sex with a view to create the appetite in the listeners. Having been worked up sexually, youths find sex irresistible and are ready to do it right away with whosoever is available. Consider a ten year old boy who sexually molested a three month old baby of a neighbour. His innocent reason was that he saw it done on the television several times so he just tried it out only to see blood all over the baby. It was the sight of blood that alerted other neighbours!

Violence is another demonic theme in modern music. Incidents of suicide and murder are sung into the minds of the listeners. This is one reason why the prisons are bulging with inmates.

Music is so powerful that young people need to be guided by their parents to know how to discern good music from bad music. A young person can choose the type of music he/she listens to if well guided and trained to do so from home by parents or guidance he/she trusts.

3. **Immoral novels and magazines**:
Satan is taking advantage of every possible avenue to lure young people into immorality. The satanic ministers are also working round the clock to pollute and confuse the hearts of the young concerning sex. Good as it is to encourage youths to be studious and read novels, caution should also be taken in determining the kind of books and magazines children are exposed to. Novels like 'Mills and Boons'' lack moral standards. It will take extra ordinary efforts for a child that is addicted to such books to remain chaste.

The Lures Of The Serpent

There are some good novels and magazines that are purely academic or entertaining and are written by morally upright authors. These kinds of materials can be given to children to read. It is better for parents to vet the novels and magazines their children read. Sometimes, they collect these materials from their friends. Parents should be close enough to their children to be able to know the kind of book diets they are feeding on or swallowing. Whatever a child ears, watches or reads will definitely define that child's character. The same even goes for the adults.

When children are well guided and they understand why it is not good to read certain books and magazines, they will not be easily enticed by friends to read such corrupt materials.

4. **Internet:**
In the olden days, researchers complained of insufficient information. In this modern day, with the advent of the internet, researchers are complaining of too much information. The internet is a very good invention. Virtually everything can now be carried out over the internet like mailing, studying, selling, buying, storing of information, preaching, adverts, etc.

On the other hand, Satan is equally using the internet to lure people especially the youths into immorality. Because of easy accessibility to the internet, pornography has now found its way into so many homes to corrupt people's minds and promote promiscuity.

Children should not be allowed to have unfiltered access to the internet. Parents have a responsibility to find a way of knowing what their children are feeding on over the internet.

5. **Peer pressure**:
Peer pressure is another way the serpent lures youths into immorality. This is why parents have the duty to thoroughly and properly educate their children from home especially on the subject of sex. Peer pressure has to do with the force of influence from friends and colleagues to do or believe certain things. Friends and schoolmates who are sexually active are known to scorn those who are chaste. The actual fact is that they feel condemned in the presence of chaste peers and then resort to talking down on their chaste colleagues, using derogatory words like 'inexperienced', 'old fashioned', 'unexposed' etc. They take time to describe the ecstasy of sex, how pleasurable and 'normal' it is. If a

child either male or female is not informed, he/she can easily be carried away and fall to the trap. Once the chaste falls to the antics of peer pressure, those his/her peers would feel satisfied that once chaste is now like them and is in no way any longer special or different.

However, when a child is made to see the importance of his/her virginity and also made to see reasons why the virginity should be kept till the wedding night, the effect of peer pressure would not be much on him/her. The child would have appropriate answers for his/her peers who are trying to mount pressures on him/her to be like them. The child would neither be in a state of confusion nor feel odd among his/her peers.

Satan depends largely on ignorance of men to confuse and defeat them morally. When a child has the right knowledge, Satan will definitely not be able to confuse that child even through his/her peers. Satan can't match a man with adequate knowledge in a contest.

6. **Inquisitiveness**:
Children are largely inquisitive. They want to know everything. This is why they ask a lot of questions. When

children ask questions and parents provide honest answers, the children learn. Answering children's questions also promotes intimacy between children and parents. However, when parents shout children down instead of honestly answering their questions, the children become repulsed and may no longer bother asking the next question.

When it comes to the subject of sex, children are understandably very inquisitive. They want to know early enough how children are born, what leads to pregnancy and through what channel the baby in the womb comes out. These are common questions children ask because they want to know. The age of a child also determines the depth of his questions.

As children grow into adolescence, they start having changes in their bodies and keep wondering what is happening. This is the reason why parents need to be close to their children in order to explain these changes to them. During and after puberty, children do have serious sexual urges. This is a very tempting time and there is need for parental guidance and tutoring for self control. When children are left to themselves to guess what is happening to them, they turn to their peers or the internet to find the answers. Satan is already waiting anxiously outside the home to lead unguided children into temptations and deliver them into evil.

Parental guidance means the parents are there for their children to appreciate their inquisitiveness and provide sincere and honest answers for them to know the appropriate things to do about their feelings. Children really wish to learn from their parents because they know their parents were once like them. They also will naturally trust their parents than any other person especially if they have confidence in their parents' explanations. When parents lie to a child, the day the child discovers the truth and realizes that his/her parents lied, that child will find it difficult to trust his/her parents again. This is why parents should always provide honest and sincere answers. If a parent does not have the answer to a question, the parent should let the child know the true position with a promise to search for the answer sooner or later. This is very important to build confidence between parents and children. When a child is confident about his parents, all things being equal, he will hide nothing from them.

Children's inquisitiveness is a good trait put into them by God because that is the way they learn naturally. It is only when parents are not there for their children early enough that the gift of inquisitiveness leads children to acquire wrong information about themselves and their feelings. This eventually leads to sin and many errors, the scars of which the child may never forget or recover from for the rest of his/her life. Parents should therefore brace up and stand up to their duties over their children by guiding them rightly to become morally upright persons.

7. **Need for love, care and cash**:
Every child needs love and care from conception. By the time they become teenagers, they become conscious of their need for cash especially, female children.

Until children leave the comfort of their parents' home, it is the responsibility of their parents to provide these three needs for them. When love and care is lacking at home, a child will look for it elsewhere and desperately too. If a child, especially a girl whose parents never told her nice words hears a few nice words from a boy, she will natural do anything for the boy just to keep hearing those nice words. Even if the boy never really meant what he was saying, for the fact that the girl had been starved of love and care from home, she is going to feel on top of the world only to find herself at the lowest ebb just a few moments after the boy had gotten what he was really looking for. It is very difficult for a girl who is used to hearing nice words from her parents to be swept off her feet by a randy lover boy.

Love and care for children means showing affection and meeting the emotional needs of a child. Children need to be hugged, pat on the back, cracked jokes with, and listened to for their complaints even in the midst of executing the parental responsibility of providing discipline.

As soon as children need to buy things for themselves, it is healthy for parents to either provide those things or empower them financially to purchase those things they need for their personal upkeep and hygiene. When children are starved of cash, the boy child may take to stealing while the girl may feel compelled to prostitute her body for cash. There are so many disgruntled elderly men outside there who are ready to spoil an innocent girl with money just to have sex with her.

While researching on the word 'virginity' over the internet, I came across the site of a girl who placed an advert over the internet to auction her virginity. Many male visitors to her site were offering huge sums of money to disvirgin her. They were requesting for information about her physique such as the size of her breasts and other lewd questions. Her site was said to have been receiving visitors every minute! She claimed she needed the money to offset her school fees. Amazingly her father was said to be a medical doctor. I really wondered why her parents could not foot the bills for her education. Reading further on the girl, I discovered she is eighteen years old and a lesbian. I shook my head and wondered what has become of this generation? Most likely, she must have been in a disagreement with her parents over her being a lesbian. Or amazingly, her parents may really not care since she is now an 'adult'. The big question is: "what moral foundation did her parents laid for her while still under their care?" May the lord have mercy! The girl eventually got a 44-year old, divorcee and father of two as the winner of her virginity auction for $20,500.

Another girl, a 22-year-old student from San Diego, California is currently in the vanity market to offer her virginity for sale. Over 10,000 men already bided for her 'ware'. The daily telegraph reported few weeks ago that the price has hit $ 3.7 million. Currently, an Australian man is said to be leading the on-line bidding at $ 5 million. There is still a good lesson to learn from this evil. The lesson is that if over 10,000 men are striving to pay millions of U.S. dollars to be the first man in a girl's life sexually, then it shows how golden, virginity is in the heart of men generally. Girls who fling this golden present carelessly are oblivious of how precious what they have is. Virginity is never an item that is meant to be sold. Human beings are fond of changing the use of God's creation into something else to fulfil their evil desires. God did not create virginity and sexuality as an item to be used to raise money. This is clearly an abuse of divine purpose. The desire of men to pay staggering amount of money for virginity goes on to confirm the divine purpose that virginity is a precious and priceless gift husband and wife should give to each other as they consummate their love on their first night in marriage.

7. Unholy lessons from older generation

Children see their parents or other elderly individuals as role models. It is amazing to note how discouraging the older generation is to the younger generation on the issue of sexual purity and morality. Children born of adulterous parents will easily be tempted to practice what they see their parents do. In other cases, it is the influence of the aunties and uncles that lures children into the acts of immorality.

When the older generation imbibes unholy life-styles, what do they expect from the younger generation? The younger generation will surely perfect and surpass the examples they learned from them.

The highest form of leadership is leadership by example. A parent who is living an immoral life-style cannot preach morality to his/her children with authority. It is usually very difficult to hide an immoral life-style from children or spouse. Somehow, the secret will leak or something will show to expose the immorality.

A parent who wishes to provide guidance on morality to his/her children should do so first by example. If a parent's words are contrary to his/her life-style, the words will carry no weight and achieve no purpose. If however, a parent's life is an example of morality, it will be much easier for the children to understand the moral instructions they are receiving from such a parent.

The Lures Of The Serpent

Parents should also do their best to make sure their children are not close to uncles/aunties who are known to be morally bankrupt. If necessary care is not taken, such uncles and aunties may become the coach employed by Satan to such children. Many uncles and aunties had introduced their nephews and nieces to the trade of immoral life-styles without the knowledge of their parents. A man cannot give what he does not have. A man can only give what he has. If some uncles/aunties are known to be flirts, parents should distance their children from having close contact or relationship with them.

4

The Consequences
Of Defilement

The youths had been made to believe that there is nothing wrong with sexual experimentation and that virginity is old fashioned. Today, some children from twelve to thirteen years of age are already disvirgined. What happens then on the wedding night? Most couples are therefore, not having their first sexual experiences on the wedding night. This is against divine ordinance. It's like God's laws are only good for the olden days. The modern man has no time for religion? Except man goes back to the basics concerning sex, the home will continue to face more degradations with attending severe consequences on the society.

There are consequences of sexual defilement. It is not true that since 'everybody' is doing it, there are no serious consequences. When divine instructions are not followed, things don't happen as ordained by God. There are consequences of sexual defilement for boys and girls. Boys had been made to believe that all the consequences of premarital sex (If any) are borne by girls. This is far from the truth. There are consequences for the boys too. The safest haven is to maintain sexual purity.

"Marriage is honourable in all, and the bed undefiled: but whoremongers and adulterers God will judge" **(Heb 13:4)**

The marriage bed should not be defiled according to God's instruction. Premarital sex is therefore a defilement of the marriage bed. Sex is meant for the married and not in any way for the unmarried. When the unmarried indulges in sex, he/she becomes defiled. Several things that ought not to be then begin to happen to such persons. Those are the consequence of sexual defilement.

A. Consequences of sexual defilement on boys

1. Sexual addiction:

The Consequences Of Defilement

Once a boy falls to the temptation of sexual experimentation, to stop becomes very difficult. The battle against the first time is the toughest for the tempter and the easiest for the tempted to win. Once a boy losses that battle, it takes much more efforts to resist subsequent temptations.

Once a boy finds it difficult to resist sexual temptations, he is hooked on sex. Sexual addiction is a very bad thing. Such boys don't see anything else in a woman than sex. Their sight and sense of judgement become blurred. They are ready to follow anything in skirts.

In marriage, the story is different. Sex is good, holy and edifying. A man can have sex with his wife for as many times as they both please. The man rightly becomes addicted to his wife who is always available for him. In marriage there is no guilt for having sex with one's partner. Sex is legal and divinely approved in marriage.

A boy who indulges in premarital sex is waking up love before it's time. This is calling for trouble!

2. **Stealing**

It is a known fact that most boys resort to acts of lying and stealing to satisfy the financial demands of their girl friends.

Especially for a boy who is addicted to sex, he will do anything to raise some cash to use in enticing girls for the purpose of taking them to bed. Bad habits beget bad habits.

When I was in the university, I knew of boys who usually stole their mothers' jewelleries to sell at school in order to live big and be nice guys to their girl friends. Some gold dealers usually visited the campus at the beginning of the semester to buy jewelleries from those boys. Stealing definitely is not a good habit.

3. **Risk of diseases**

Sexually transmitted diseases are common among youths because they usually have multiple sexual partners. The risk of contracting HIV/AIDS is also there. In spite of the reliance on condom, people are still contacting HIV/AIDS through Sex. The condom is not all that dependable after all. Why should a boy who has a future hang his destiny on the balance of the performance of one imperfect condom that can easily burst or leak?

Many have lost their lives to the pleasure of premarital sex. Life is full of choices and I believe that it is better to choose life than death. Any pleasure that has the possibility of sicknesses or death is not a good choice for a wise man.

4. Early fathering

This world is full of babies, fathering and mothering babies. Premarital sex can lead to unwanted pregnancies which in turn can lead to early fathering. Early fathering sometimes becomes a stumbling block on the way of progress. It is an unnecessary distraction at a time a boy is still taking steps to becoming a man. The shame, disappointment to parents and emotional traumas are also there.

5. Probable loss of future plans

When a boy can't get help from parents or relatives to assist him in shouldering his responsibilities as an early father, he might be forced out of school in order to stand up to his new responsibility. This usually resorts to a loss of a glorious future plan. In some years to come, the difference between him and his peers will become clear. What regrets and pity become the lots of such men?

If a young man can deny himself of pleasures while investing into his future, nothing else can stop him from having his desired future and destiny.

6. Loss of sexual satisfaction in marriage

I have heard it said that a man should please himself sexually with as many sexual partners as he desires before getting married so that after marriage, he can settle down with his wife alone. Unfortunately, the contrary is true in most cases. How can a man who is used to multiple sexual partners now settle down for only one woman just because he is married to her?

It takes only a change of heart through a spiritual encounter with God to change sexual habits. Once a man's sexual taste bud is adjusted to multiple partners, it becomes very difficult to just change that overnight. So, premarital sex also adversely affects future sexual satisfaction in marriage.

7. Spiritual contamination

Sex is not just a physical affair. It is also a spiritual affair. A man becomes spiritually contaminated as he jumps from one woman to the other. Spiritual contamination leads to spiritual problems. The only remedy for this is salvation in Christ and appropriate deliverance.

The spiritual determines the physical. Once spiritually contaminated, the physical can't be free of troubles. Sex is both a physical and a spiritual union. Both sex partners partake of each other's spiritual conditions through sex.

8. **Demonic possession**

Many had not only been spiritually contaminated through sex, they had also become demon possessed.

"What? Know ye not that he which is joined to an harlot is one body? For two saith he, shall be one flesh" (I Cor. 6: 16)

When a girl is demon possessed, and a boy sleeps with her, the demons can freely and legally cross from the girl's body into the boy's body and vice versa. From that day, the boy is in trouble. The demons will reside in his body and torment him in several ways. It is only the power in the name of Jesus that can cast out such demons.

Demonic possession sometimes can result into sicknesses or ill-luck. Demons also like to exercise control over the life of their hosts. They want to determine what happens to the man. They usually bring calamities and woes with the intent to steal, kill and destroy. Many men with a glorious future had thereby been reduced to a mere piece of bread! That means a loss of value in life.

B. Consequences of sexual defilement on girls

1. Loss of a golden present

A girl cannot truly be a virgin twice. Once she is sexually defiled, she loses her virginity. No matter how she regrets her actions, the virginity is gone forever. This is a loss of a golden present which is meant for her husband. Once this golden present is lost, money, tears, regrets or lying cannot restore it.

If you now know how important your virginity is to your future marriage, please do all you can to keep it if you still have it. If however you have lost it, be open to your future husband about it. Don't hide the truth from him. When found out, the shame of hiding the truth is worse than the 'shame' of saying the truth. The truth shall set you free.

2. Loss of self esteem

Once a girl is sexually defiled, her self esteem goes down. She knows she is no longer a chaste girl. She has become a package already tampered with. Even when people around still hold her in high esteem, she reduces in self esteem in her own sight as soon as she remembers what happened. Afterwards, her bargaining power reduces until it comes to zero. She finds herself giving in to more boys since there is nothing she is 'defending' again. The sweetness of sex in itself also becomes highly indulging that it becomes difficult to stop. That is why it is better to remain chaste. It is better not to taste sex until the right time (in marriage) in order to avoid sexual addiction and confusion. A trial does confuse.

A girl who has kept herself chaste will always be on guard to 'defend' herself. She won't allow any boy to mess around with her. It's easier for chaste girls to find genuine lovers instead of just being used and dumped by all sorts of men.

3. Teenage pregnancy

Premarital sex usually leads to teenage pregnancy. Once a girl starts seeing her monthly period, she can be pregnant if sexually active. Teenage pregnancy is a sorry sight to behold. The teenage girl's life can never be the same again. It's either the girl chooses to abort the pregnancy not minding the attending consequences or have the baby. Abortion sometimes leads to death, barrenness and guilty conscience. If the teenage girl opts to have the baby, she then needs to come face to face with some realities. She may not be physically strong to go through labour and when she eventually has the baby, she has suddenly become a mother.

What then happens to her future plans? Whichever path she chooses, there are dire consequences.

4. Single parenting

It is most likely that a teenage boy who impregnated another teenage girl will not accept responsibility for the child. Even where the boy accepts responsibility, he still cannot responsibly father a child at this stage of his life. Most times, the girl becomes a single parent in her parents' house.

Single parenting is no joke. It's better for a girl to do without the experience as much as possible. Sexual purity and chastity is the way out.

5. Shame

When a school girl becomes pregnant without being married, she can't be proud of herself. She will feel ashamed and hide from the public as much as she could. Why risk a possible life of shame instead of saying a simple no?

6. Defeat

Men are conquering oriented. Many girls feel if they give themselves sexually to a boy, the boy will love them and marry them. This is very far from the truth. Once a boy 'conquers' a girl sexually, he is no longer as excited as he used to be about the girl. In fact, he is already looking for new 'territories' to conquer.

However, if the girl refuses to give herself sexually until marriage, the boy will do everything including going through the rigours of a wedding ceremony at the right time to 'conquer' the girl if he truly loves her.

Premarital sex cheapens a girl. It puts the girl at a disadvantage. Most ladies who give in to premarital sex usually are the ones running after the man and begging him to marry them!

7. **Slimmer chances of marriage**

Premarital sex slims down a woman's chances of getting a choice suitor to marry. A lady who already had a child by mistake may not easily find a man of her dream to marry any longer. Most men who never married will not like to marry a lady who already had a child for someone.

Many men also will not like to marry a girl they know had been passed around so well. They may also approach her for sex, but definitely not for marriage. At the end of the day, such a girl may have to settle down for whosoever is available, not her real choice of a man or desire of an husband.

We all have this one life to live. After here, it is eternity. It is better to live and discipline oneself in such a way as to have the best out of life. It's never fulfilling to settle down for the second or third best when the best is possible. As you lay your bed, so will you lie on it?

8. Future tears

Some mistakes are not possible to correct. Premarital sex sometimes leads to future tears. Many women are still secretly shedding the tears of the mistakes they made in their youths. Many women who ought to have become one of the movers and shakers of the society are today hedged-in into a corner because they chose to do the right thing at the wrong time. Each time they see their peers who did the right things at the right time, they feel sorrowful and shed tears. No matter how they receive encouraging words they still feel the pain. Some other women are married today but can't get pregnant because of several abortions in the past. The pain for such category of waiting mothers is usually excruciating. May be in their own time, nobody told them of the possible consequences of their actions.

Now that the knowledge is there, a better performance is expected.

9. Risk of venereal diseases and HIV/AIDS

Sexual activities, especially with more than one partner put a girl at the risk of venereal diseases and the dreaded HIV/AIDS. Many of those boys don't stay with one sexual partner. Even if the girl keeps only him, she still stands the risk of contacting venereal diseases and HIV/AIDS because the boy is not keeping only her.

Some venereal diseases can lead to other complications if not treated on time. HIV/AIDS had killed millions of youths who refused to control themselves sexually. Life is worth more than dying for sex.

10. Spiritual contamination

Premarital sex and multiple sexual partners lead to spiritual contaminations. Sex is not only a physical thing. It is also a spiritual affair. Each sexual partner makes a spiritual deposit into the other, which leads to spiritual contaminations. Spiritual contamination leads to spiritual problems like bad dreams, ill-luck and spiritual afflictions. A girl can always do without all these rubbish by staying chaste.

11. Demonic possession

Risk of demonic possession is very sure through illicit sexual intercourse. A man and a woman are one spiritually when having sex. At this time, demons can cross over from one partner to the other. Demonic possession is a serious spiritual problem. Demons usually torment their host bodies. Only the power in the name of Jesus can cast them out and destroy their powers.

5
The Divine Connection

God understands our frailties and he is ready to help us. There is a divine connection to our victory over sin. Sexual sin is such an enticing sin that if the divine connection is missing, it might be very difficult to overcome.

God made man with the sex drive. If really, God does not intend man to have sex until marriage, then he must have a plan for the unmarried to contain the burning sexual desire in their bodies.

God made man without sin, but with an ability to choose either good or bad. This is called the power of the will. Man was created as a free moral being. God does not choose for man. He rather prefers man to choose for himself.

The Beauty Of Virginity

God's perfect plan for man is for man to be in a relationship with Him, follow His instructions and receive His spirit into himself. The Holy Spirit in a man helps the man where he is weak and assists the man to see clearly in order to choose rightly. The Holy Spirit in a man also neutralizes the powers of evil which tries to compel a man to choose evil. When a man enters into a relationship with God, the power of evil over the man's life is broken.

"For sin shall not have dominion over you: for ye are not under the law, but under grace".
(Rom. 6:14)

The power of sin actually dominates a man's life until he finds salvation in Christ and that power of sin is broken. For the unsaved, there is a spiritual atmosphere around him that blindfolds and compels him to take the decision to sin. The unsaved is still under the bondage of sin. For the saved, that dark spiritual atmosphere is destroyed at salvation. The saved is not being blindfolded or compelled to sin. If the saved sins, he did so in spite of his spiritual liberty and all that he knows. The unsaved mind cannot assimilate the word of God. He desires to choose the good, but does not know what is really good for him. He lives in a state of spiritual confusion:

The Divine Connection

"But if our gospel be hid, it is hid to them that are lost: In whom the god of this world hath blinded the minds of them which believe not, lest the light of the glorious gospel of Christ, who is the image of God, should shine unto them" (2 Cor. 4:3-4)

When a man embraces the truth of the gospel and gets converted, he can then see and be guided by the light of the word of God. Those who reject the salvation Christ offers are lost. They are groping in darkness and can't find their way. They lie, cheat and fornicate with impunity. Their conscience becomes dead over time as they continue to do those things which are not convenient

"And even as they did not like to retain God in their knowledge, God gave them over to a reprobate mind, to do those things which are not convenient; Being filled with all unrighteousness, fornication, wickedness, covetousness ..." (Rom 1: 28 - 29)

The divine connection to the preservation of virginity or chastity is to be born again and obey the instructions of the word of God.

The Beauty Of Virginity

"My son, attend to my words; incline thine ear unto my sayings let them not depart from thine eyes; keep them in the midst of thine heart. For they are life unto those that find them, and health to all their flesh" **(Prov. 4: 20-22)**

Parents should be born again and then lead their children to Christ. When this is done, the issue of morality becomes much easier to deal with.

If you want to give your life to Jesus Christ and get born again, say this prayer aloud after me:

O God, I thank you for speaking to my heart. I also thank you for sending your son Jesus Christ to die for my sins. I know I am a sinner. I repent from my sins and ask that you forgive me all my sins and iniquity. From today, I surrender my life to you. Thank you for saving me. In Jesus' name I pray (Amen).

Now that you have said this prayer by faith, God has answered your prayer. Your sins are now forgiven and your name is hereby written in the book of life. You can write me for more instructions. You should also look for a church of your choice where people are encouraged to be born again and start attending. God is on your side.

In case you have been born again before but still find yourself neck deep in the mire of sin, you need to rededicate your life to God. You cannot really be born of God and still be living in sin. *"**Whosoever is born of God doth not commit sin; for his seed remaineth in him: and he cannot sin, because he is born of God" (1 John 3:9).** A believer may slip or fall into sin once in a while, but he that is born of God cannot be a habitual sinner.

Break that jinx

Now that you are born again or if you had been born again, you can be free from the jinx of covenants struck through the sin of premarital or extramarital sexual relationships. Until covenants are broken, they remain in force and can be the source of untold hardships in your life and marriage. Praise God, you can now be free from the jinx of ill-luck and curses. Your being in Christ has put you in a superior covenant with the King of kings and the Lord of lords. You can follow these steps to receive your deliverance:

1. If you are married, you need to first confess to your spouse and receive his/her forgiveness in case you have

not done so before. This is because every sin of immorality is also a sin against your spouse. If you are single, you are required by God to preserve your body for your future spouse and consummate your marriage covenant with your first sexual experience with him/her. Since you are not yet married, but have indulged in premarital sex, you may just move on to step 2 to have your deliverance. Thank God you are now born again or have rededicated your life to God.

2. Go to the Lord in prayers and ask for God's forgiveness. Confess your sins of immorality to God and also receive God's forgiveness. Pray with a heart of repentance until you have peace in your heart that God has forgiven you. Ask in faith and God will surely forgive you. *"If we say that we have no sin, we deceive ourselves, and the truth is not in us. If we confess our sins, he is faithful and just to forgive us our sins, and to cleanse us from all unrighteousness" (1 John 1:8-9).*

3. Mention the names of your past sexual partners one by one and pronounce the spiritual covenants and agreements struck by your sexual intercourse with them broken in Jesus'

name. Make these pronouncements by faith. The covenants are been broken as you say so in the name of Jesus.

4. Destroy the effects of those covenants on your life and destiny by the blood of Jesus (Rev. 12:11).

5. Make up your mind never to return into the mire of sexual immorality again and forever.

6. Make a covenant with God to live pure and holy.

A beloved sister shared this testimony of her deliverance from the effects of unbroken premarital sexual covenants in her marriage:

"Since I got married, my husband and I had always been fighting. We don't use to see eye to eye on almost every issue. We've gone for several counselling sessions but the problem persisted. One day, my pastor's wife shared with some of us on the topic of breaking spiritual sexual covenants and the negative effects it can have on a marriage if remain unbroken. She said after being born again, one needs to break all the covenants with previous sexual partners with a special reference to the first sexual partner.

The Beauty Of Virginity

She added that the devil can use such unbroken covenants to launch spiritual attacks against somebody's life and marriage. I then remembered the man I had my first sexual experience with before I gave my life to Christ and met my husband. I never imagined that it was a covenant or that the experience can have any adverse effect on my marriage even after I became born again.

Consequently, I went to have a time with the lord in prayer. I mentioned the name of that man and broke whatever spiritual covenant that was established between us through sexual relationships in Jesus' name. I prayed all manners of prayers and recovered all my blessings the enemy had stolen in Jesus' name. Later on that night when I slept, I had a dream. In my dream, I saw this same man and me struggling over a machete. I had an understanding in the dream that the machete belonged to me. Eventually, I collected the machete from him and started running. He gave me a chase but could not catch up with me. Later, I saw another machete which belonged to my husband. So, I kept my own beside it and said 'iron sharpeneth iron'. Then, I woke up.

The Divine Connection

Since this incident happened, I observed that my husband suddenly changed positively towards me. Now, if I offer an advice, he listens. We now sit down together as husband and wife to make plans without fighting as we used to do. In fact, it's like we just got married! I thank God for restoring peace into my marriage through this knowledge."

6
How To Keep
Virginity Till Marriage

Even though, this world is perverted morally, there are still a handful of individuals, who are getting married as virgins. Either you have lost your virginity or not, this chapter will help you to know how to keep virginity or be chaste from now on.

1. The first thing I advice is to arrive at a decision to keep your virginity until after marriage. Decisions are very important. Once you can decide on this, you then know the direction to follow. If an idea can enter into your mind, then you can do it. No matter what others are saying or doing, once you can make up your mind to be chaste, it becomes possible. Your friends and peers will soon know you for whom you are and find their levels around you. It

is not possible to get along with everybody. Once your mind is made up, those who can be your friends are determined.

2. You should carefully select your friends. If your current friends are those who are sexually active, you might need to change them. Birds of the same feather flock together. If you hang around with your old friends too much, they will discourage you from keeping to your decision. You are permitted to change your friends. It is just a matter of time, you will soon make new friends, especially among equally born again peers. Friendship is by choice.

3. Start breaking habits that can lure you or prepare your mind for premarital sex. Give up on literatures that encourage immorality. Declare pornography as a taboo to you from henceforth. Never give it a glance again forever. Guide your heart diligently. Destroy immoral magazines from your library. If you collected such from friends, return them immediately and use it as an opportunity to advice your friends to make a decision for chastity.

4. Fellowship with God's word. Read the book of Proverbs and glean some wisdom for yourself. The word of God renews our minds as we read and meditate. Renewing our

minds means old information stored in the mind start giving way to new information found in the word of God.

5. Pray without ceasing. Pray in the spirit a great deal. Praying in the spirit (Speaking in tongues) helps our weaknesses as the Holy Spirit makes intercession for us with groaning which cannot be uttered (Rom. 8:26).

6. Understand that the act of sexual intercourse is progressive. One thing usually leads to the other. If you are in a relationship, let your partner know about your decision and refrain from activities that can lead to sex. Don't work up yourselves through passionate romance and hope to stop the progression just before the sexual act. Most times, it becomes very difficult to stop.

7. Do not enter into a relationship with someone who believes he/she cannot do without having sex before marriage. Two people cannot walk together except they are in agreement.

8. Don't put yourself in circumstances that can easily lead you to premarital sex. For example, don't stay alone behind locked doors with someone of the opposite sex or the one you are in a relationship with. Don't visit at odd times or

sleep over in the same room in his/her apartment. Do not make preparations for the flesh to fulfil its lust.

9. Don't have too long courtship. As soon as appropriate and affordable, get married. A prolonged courtship gives room for temptations.

7
Sexually Transmitted Diseases

A sexually transmitted disease (STD) is an infection passed from person to person through sexual contact. It is also called venereal diseases (VD). STDs can affect boys and girls, men and women of all ages and background who are sexually active.

The younger a person starts engaging in sex, the greater his/her chances of becoming infected with STD. Those who have sex with more than one partner have higher chances of getting infected. "STDs are more than just an embarrassment. They're a serious health problem. If untreated, some STDs can cause permanent damage, such as infertility (the inability to have a baby) and even death (in the case of HIV/AIDS)"[5]

The Beauty Of Virginity

STDs are spreading so easily because people now put their trust in condoms, believing they are playing safe. There is really nothing like a 100% safe sex except abstinence for the unmarried and faithfulness for the married. That is the script for safe sex as written by the creator. A person can get some STDs like herpes or genital warts through skin-to-skin contact with infected area or sore. The condom is not totally reliable as the failure rate is high. The condom can burst during sex without giving any warning. Many had contacted STDs and HIV that way. According to Dr McIlhaney of Medical Institute for Sexual Health, U.S.A, "The public announcements about "safe sex" infuriate me, because what they're saying is that you can safely have sex outside of marriage if you use condoms, and you don't have to worry about getting an STD. The message is a lie. The failure rate of condoms is extremely high, and that's why married people don't use them."[6]

STDs can also be transmitted through anal or Oral sex. Viruses or bacteria that cause STDs can enter the body through tiny cuts or tears in the mouth and anus, as well as the genitals. "Some STDs like Trichomoniasis can also be picked up from contact with damp or moist objects such as towels, wet clothing, or a toilet seat, if the genital area gets in contact with these damp objects"[7]

How many people have STDs?

"The rate of infection of STDs is so high. In the United States alone, about 19 Million new infections are estimated to occur each year. Women suffer more frequent and more serious complications from STDs than men"[8]

Quoting from Dr James Dobson in 'Complete Marriage and Family Home Reference Guide', "You've heard that HIV is deadly because it leads to AIDS, but the human papillomavirus (HPV) causes far more deaths among women in the U.S. each year. Thousands of American women die from it every year. It causes genital warts and in some patients leads to cancer of the cervix. In fact, it is estimated that 90 percent of cervical-cancer cases are caused by HPV, and the virus itself cannot be eradicated once it is in the system.

A medical investigation of this virus was conducted at the University of California at Berkeley in 1992. Averaging twenty-one year of age, all the young women coming to the campus health center for routine gynaecological examinations for one year were tested for HPV. Would you believe that 47 percent of these female students were found to carry this virus? Every one of them will suffer painful symptoms for the rest of their lives, and some will die of cervical and uterine cancer.

The most disturbing news is that HPV can be transmitted while the male is wearing a condom. The virus lurks around the portion of the genitalia that is not covered by the condom. This is one of the reasons some of us object strenuously to the campaign to get young people to have "protected sex". It gives them a false sense of security. There is no such thing as safe sex when it occurs promiscuously and outside the marital relationship. Abstinence before marriage is the only safe way to go."[9]

Speaking on the effects of the failure of the safe-sex advocates, Dr McIlhaney was quoted by Dr Dobson: "I see the examples of these failures in my office every day. These include victims of Chlamydia, probably the most prevalent STD, and of human papilloma virus (HPV), which can cause a lasting irritation of the female organs, as well as cancer of the vulva, vagina, and cervix. It is one of the most difficult diseases to treat and kills more than 4,800 women a year. I also see victims of herpes, which some studies indicates is present in up to 30-40 percent of single, sexually active people, as well as victims of syphilis, which is at a forty-year high" [10]

It is unfortunate that we don't have enough published statistics in the developing countries on STDs, but I personally believe the rate is more staggering because of exposure to poverty and lack of adequate medical care. Quoting A.O.Osoba from the British Journal Of Venereal Diseases' website, "At present very little information is available on the prevalence and pattern of sexually transmitted diseases (STDs) in many countries of tropical Africa. The available evidence does, however, suggest that these diseases are highly prevalent and that a considerable reservoir of infection exists among the female population. Gonorrhoea is probably the most commonly recognized STD in tropical Africa, frequently causing epididymitis and urethral stricture in men and salpingitis and pelvic inflammatory disease in women. The prevalence of a infectious syphilis is still high, particularly the late manifestations of the disease. The prevalence of the other STDs is also high. Thus, the problem is clearly very serious and the need for improving facilities for diagnosis and treatment urgent; some attempt also must be made to initiate control measures."[11]

A study was made between March and April, 1997 on selected secondary school students in Benin City, Nigeria. 510 randomly selected students were interviewed, using a structured questionnaire based on qualitative research. Average age was 18 years (14-29 range). A multivariable logistic regression model was used to identify independent determinants of STDs. RESULTS: Of the 65% of respondents who reported sexual intercourse experience, 40% of girls and 29% of boys reported ever having had a STD. Methods used to prevent STDs included condoms (43%), abstinence (17%), fewer partners (14%), no protection (12%), and traditional medicine (4%). In practice, no condom use was reported by 24% of sexually active youth. Sources of STD treatment were: "chemists" (over the counter drug stores) (22%), no treatment (19%), private physician (16%), public clinic (8%), self treatment (8%), traditional healers (3%), and other (8%). Reasons for not using public STD clinics were: cost (58%), privacy (46%), feeling guilty at clinics (42%), long wait time (14%), and poor medicinal effectiveness (8%). 29% of youth were unaware that sex while experiencing a STD symptom could spread the infection, and 25% reported that adolescents do have sex while experiencing STD symptoms. [12]

In a recent study conducted by The Women's Health & Action Research Center, an NGO based in Nigeria, on "The health-seeking behaviour of in-school adolescents in Nigeria", it was discovered that: "Available evidence suggests that there is a high rate of sexually transmitted diseases (STDs) among Nigerian adolescents. Despite the high rate of STDs among Nigerian adolescents, it has been recognized that many adolescents either do not receive treatment or receive inadequate treatment for various STDs. It is conceivable that the lack of proper treatment of STDs is one of the factors that maintain the high rate of infection among adolescents, and contributes to high HIV transmission in the country." [13]

I believe the situation is getting worse by the day. More and more young people are experimenting with sex. In the above studies, we were told that 24% of sexually active youths don't even use the condom. Of the rest that use condom, a good percentage will have accidents (condom bursting or perforation) while the rest will still get infected with STDs that condoms cannot prevent. Young people are increasingly becoming sexually active because abstinence had been played down while the use of condom had been greatly emphasized. The summary of what young people make out of the ABC approach is: "You can have sex if you want, but use condom if you're smart". This way, young people no longer exercise any restrain towards sex. They feel it is normal, everybody is doing it and that parents even expect them to do it. Until we start saying the truth as it ought to be by deemphasizing the use of condom and emphasizing abstinence, more and more youths will keep contacting sexually transmitted diseases with attending serious consequences for them now and in their adult lives?

SOME COMMON STDS, THEIR SYMPTOMS AND IMPLICATIONS

Chlamydia

Chlamydia is a common STD with over 1 million cases reported yearly in the U.S. The actual number is higher because not every of STD is usually reported. In Africa, I wonder how many millions get infected every year. Among all age groups, teens and young adults have the highest rate of infection.

Sexually Transmitted Diseases

Chlamydia is a curable infection caused by the bacteria Chlamydia trachomatis. It can be transmitted through sexual intercourse. "Most women with Chlamydia (and about half of men) do not experience symptoms. If symptoms do occur, they usually appear 1 to 3 weeks after infection".[14] A person can transmit Chlamydia to a sexual partner from the time of infection (when he/she may be ignorant of the infection) until the time treatment is completed and successful.

Some of the symptoms of Chlamydia include: Genital discharge, burning when urinating, bleeding between menstrual periods, lower abdominal pain, low back pain, nausea, fever, pain during sex.

If left untreated, Chlamydia can lead to complications such as Pelvic Inflammatory Disease (PID) and infertility.

Genital herpes

Genital herpes is a sexually transmitted disease caused by the *herpes simplex viruses* (HSV) type 1 and type 2. Most genital herpes is caused by HSV type 2.

Most people have no or minimal symptoms from HSV-1 or HSV-2 infection. When symptoms do occur, they usually appear as one or more blisters on or around the genitals or rectum. The blisters break, leaving ulcers or tender sores that may take up to four weeks to heal. Typically, another outbreak can appear weeks or months later. [15]

Sexual herpes can be transmitted through sexual contacts with an infected person. Condom is not effective against transmission to another person especially when there are open sores. Just a body contact with an open sore can effect a transmission. Genital herpes can also be transmitted either the infected person has open sores or not.

Genital herpes is a very common disease since it can be transmitted even when the infected person is not yet aware that he/she has it. Others who had been treated and the open sores have disappeared may think they no longer have it and keep transferring the virus to other people ignorantly. "About 45 million Americans, age 12 and older have genital herpes. It's estimated that up to one million people become infected each year. Genital Herpes (HSV-2) is more common in women than men." [16] Even though, we don't have published statistics of STD infections here in Nigeria, doctors are testifying that the rate is very high and alarming! There is no treatment that can cure genital herpes. The sores may disappear or reappear, but the virus remains in the body. Once you have the virus, it stays in your body. However, there are drugs you can use to shorten or stop the intervals of outbreaks from happening.

Genital herpes is a lifelong disease. If you had it once, it will always be in your body. Even if you don't have outbreaks for a long time, the virus is still there. Anytime you have an outbreak, consult your doctor for treatment. Also let your doctor advice you and prescribe drugs you can use to prevent or stop regular outbreaks.

If you are already married, discuss the disease with your spouse so that he/she can go for testing and probably treatment. Don't have sex when you have outbreaks.

Genital herpes can cause problems during pregnancy and breast-feeding. According to information available on Women's Health Information Center's website:

"If the mother is having her first outbreak while she is pregnant, she is more likely to pass the virus to her baby. If the outbreak is not the first one, the baby's risk of getting the virus is very low. Babies born with herpes may be premature or may die, or they may have brain damage, severe rashes, or eye problems. Doctors may do a C-section to deliver a baby if the mother has herpes lesions near the birth canal to help prevent passing the virus. Also, *acyclovir* can help babies born with herpes if they are treated right away.

It is not yet known if all genital herpes drugs are safe for pregnant women to take. Some doctors may recommend *acyclovir* be taken either as a pill or through an IV (a needle into a vein) during pregnancy. Let your doctor know if you have genital herpes, even if you are not having an outbreak. He or she will help you manage it safely during pregnancy. If you have genital herpes, you can keep breast-feeding as long as the sores are covered. Herpes is spread through contact with sores and can be dangerous to a newborn. If you have sores on your nipple or areola, the darker skin around the nipple, you should stop breast-feeding on that breast. Pump or hand express your milk from that breast until the sore clears. Pumping will help keep up your milk supply and prevent your breast from getting engorged or overly full. You can store your milk to give to your baby in a bottle at another feeding. If the parts of your breast pump that contact the milk also touch the sore(s) while pumping, you should throw the milk away." [17]

Some of the symptoms of genital herpes include: Itching or burning feeling in the genital or anal area, fever, headache, muscle aches, pain when urinating, genital discharge, small red bumps, blisters, or open sores on the penis, vagina, or on areas close by, burning, or swollen glands in genital area, pain in legs, buttocks, or genital area. Symptoms of genital herpes are worse in AIDS patients.

Gonorrhea

Gonorrhea is a curable infection caused by the bacteria 'Neisseria gonorrhoea'. Gonorrhoea typically spread during sexual intercourse. It can also be passed from infected mothers to their new born infants during delivery. This causes conjunctivitis (eye infection) which, if left untreated can lead to blindness. [18]

The U.S. Centers for Disease Control and Prevention (CDC) estimates that approximately 700,000 new gonorrheal infections occur yearly in the U.S., only about half of which are reported to the CDC. More than 5% of people between the ages of 18 and 35 have an infection with gonorrhea that they do not know about. New strains are more easily spread and are resisting treatment even with strong antibiotics. [19]

The Beauty Of Virginity

Many men infected with gonorrhea exhibit symptoms, while most women are asymptomatic (without symptoms). Even when women do have symptoms, they can be mistaken for a bladder infection or other virginal infection. In men, symptoms usually appear within 2-7 days after infection, with a possible range of 1 to 30 days. Women who develop infection may do so within 10 days of infection. A person with gonorrhea is able to transmit the infection from the time infected till treatment is successful.

Some of the symptoms of gonorrhea are: Pain or burning when urinating, yellowish and sometimes bloody genital discharge, bleeding between menstrual periods.

Gonorrhea can be very dangerous if it is left untreated, even in someone who has mild or no symptoms. In girls, the infection can move into the uterus, fallopian tubes, and ovaries (causing PID) and can lead to scarring and infertility (the inability to have a baby). Gonorrhea infection during pregnancy can cause problems for the newborn baby, including meningitis (an inflammation of the membranes around the brain and spinal cord) and an eye infection that can result in blindness if it is not treated.

<u>Sexually Transmitted Diseases</u>

In guys, gonorrhea can spread to the epididymis (the structure attached to the testicle that helps transport sperm), causing pain and swelling in the testicular area. This can create scar tissue that might make a guy infertile. In both guys and girls, untreated gonorrhea can affect other organs and parts of the body including the throat, eyes, heart, brain, skin, and joints, although this is less common.[20]

Hepatitis
Hepatitis is an inflammation of the liver that can be caused by some of viruses. There are five major types of hepatitis i.e. Hepatitis A, B, C, D & E.

Hepatitis A is mainly transmitted through contamination with blood or stool of an infected person. The hepatitis B virus (HBV) can be transmitted through sexual intercourse or if a person's mucus membranes or blood are exposed to an infected person's blood, saliva, semen or vaginal secretions. Hepatitis C is transmitted through contamination with an infected person's blood. Hepatitis D infects people with active hepatitis B, while hepatitis E is spread mainly through fecal contamination of water supplies or food. Sexual activity is most closely associated with hepatitis B. Hepatitis can be a silent killer as there may be no symptom in some cases, until the liver cells are damaged. When hepatitis viruses damage liver cells, scar tissue is formed and those cells can no longer function. With fewer healthy liver cells, the body begins to show symptoms ranging from mild (such as fatigue) to more severe symptoms (such as mental confusion). [21]

Hepatitis A and B are preventable through vaccination. No vaccination currently exists for hepatitis C or E. Since hepatitis D only infects persons with active hepatitis B, the vaccine for hepatitis B prevents D. [22] The vaccines protects against the virus in more than 95% of cases for 10 years. [23]

Some of the symptoms of Hepatitis B include: mild fever, headache and muscle aches, tiredness, loss of appetite, nausea or vomiting, diarrhea, dark-colored urine and pale bowel movements, stomach pain, skin and whites of eyes turning yellow. [24]

Hepatitis can lead to death if not treated on time. [23]

HIV and AIDS
Human Immunodeficiency Virus (HIV) is a viral infection which destroys the immune system. The immune system is

the body's ability to fight off viruses, bacteria and fungi that cause disease. HIV makes the human body more susceptible to certain types of cancers and to infections the body would normally resist, such as pneumonia and meningitis. The virus and the infection itself are known as HIV. When HIV has caused havoc to the body's immune system, it then progresses to a later stage know as "Acquired immunodeficiency syndrome (AIDS)".

HIV is transmitted through direct contact of a mucous membrane or the bloodstream with a bodily fluid containing HIV, such as blood, semen, vaginal fluid, preseminal fluid, and breast milk. This transmission can involve anal, vaginal or oral sex, blood transfusion, contaminated hypodermic needles, exchange between mother and baby during pregnancy, childbirth, or breast-feeding, or other exposure to one of the above bodily fluids.[25]

An estimated 39.5 million people have HIV worldwide. And though the spread of the virus has slowed in some countries, it has escalated or remained unchanged in others. The best hope for stemming the spread of HIV lies in prevention, treatment and education.[26]

The Beauty Of Virginity

At present, no cure had been found for HIV/AIDS. AIDS is now a pandemic. In 2007, it was estimated to have killed about 2.1 million people worldwide, including 330,000 children. Over three-quarters of these deaths occurred in sub-Saharan Africa, retarding economic growth and destroying human capital. [27]

Opportunistic infections are common in people with AIDS. HIV affects nearly every organ system. People with AIDS also have an increased risk of developing various cancers such as Kaposi's sarcoma, cervical cancer and cancers of the immune system known as lymphomas. Additionally, people with AIDS often have systemic symptoms of infection like frequent low-grade fevers and night sweats, swollen glands, chills, weakness, and rapid weight loss. The specific opportunistic infections that AIDS patients develop depend in part on the prevalence of these infections in the geographic area in which the patient lives. Other symptoms of HIV/AIDS include: Extreme fatigue, frequent yeast infections (in the mouth), vaginal yeast infections and other STDs, pelvic inflammatory disease (PID), menstrual cycle changes, red, brown, or purplish blotches on or under the skin or inside the mouth, nose, or eyelids.

Sexually Transmitted Diseases

AIDS had killed millions worldwide and many are still dying daily. Although treatments for AIDS and HIV can slow the course of the disease, there is currently no vaccine or cure. Antiretroviral treatment reduces both the mortality and the morbidity of HIV infection, but these drugs are expensive and routine access to antiretroviral medication is not available in all countries. Due to the difficulty in treating HIV infection, preventing infection is a key aim in controlling the AIDS epidemic, with health organizations promoting safe sex and needle-exchange programs in attempts to slow the spread of the virus.[28] Thanks for efforts of safe-sex advocates so far. The best approach to prevent this killer disease is abstinence and mutual faithfulness in marriage.

Pubic lice (Crabs)
Pubic lice, also known as crabs are small parasites that feed on human blood. Pubic lice are not the same as head and body lice. Crabs are usually found on the pubic hair, armpits and eyelashes. Crabs rarely infest head hair.

A person can get pubic lice during sexual contact with an infected person. Crabs can be sexually transmitted even if there is no penetration or exchange of body fluids. Crabs can move from the pubic hair of one person to the pubic hair of another. Animals do not get crabs.

The most noticeable symptom of crabs is itching and finding lice. The itching usually starts five days after a person gets infected. The only way to prevent infection with crabs is avoid contact with infected people, bed linens, clothing, and furniture. [29]

Latex condom cannot prevent pubic lice.

Syphilis

Syphilis is a sexually transmitted disease caused by the spirochetal bacterium Treponema pallidum subspecies *pallidum*. The route of transmission of syphilis is almost always through sexual contact, although there are examples of congenital syphilis via transmission from mother to fetus in the womb.

The signs and symptoms of syphilis are numerous; before the advent of serological testing, precise diagnosis was very difficult. In fact, the disease was dubbed the "Great Imitator" because it was often confused with other diseases, particularly in its tertiary stage.[30] Sir William Osler stated, "The physician who knows syphilis knows medicine."[31] Symptoms: A single, painless sore appears, usually in the genital areas but may appear in the mouth. If infection is not treated, it moves to the next stage.

Symptoms in the next, or secondary, stage are: skin rash on the hands and feet that usually does not itch and clears on its own, fever, swollen lymph glands, sore throat, patchy hair loss, headaches, weight loss, muscle aches, tiredness.

In the latent, or hidden, stage, the symptoms listed above disappear, but the symptoms from the second stage can come back. In the late stage, infection remains in the body and can damage the brain, nerves, eyes, heart, blood vessels, liver, bones, and joints.[32]

Tertiary syphilis usually occurs 1-10 years after the initial infection, though in some cases it can take up to 50 years. This stage is characterized by the formation of gummas which are soft, tumor-like balls of inflammation known as granulomas. The granulomas are chronic and represent an inability of the immune system to completely clear the organism. They may appear almost anywhere in the body including in the skeleton. The gummas produce a chronic inflammatory state in the body with mass-effects upon the local anatomy. Other characteristics of untreated tertiary syphilis include neuropathic joint disease, which is a degeneration of joint surfaces resulting from loss of sensation and fine position sense (proprioception). The more severe manifestations include neurosyphilis and cardiovascular syphilis. In a study of untreated syphilis, 10% of patients developed cardiovascular syphilis, 16% had gumma formation, and 7% had neurosyphilis. [33]

To avoid syphilis, abstain from sex or be mutually faithful in marriage. If you choose to practice a promiscuous safe sex, you may not be that lucky. God's ways are still the best.

Trichomoniasis
Trichomoniasis, sometimes referred to as "trich", is a common cause of vaginitis. It results both from shared external water sources (hot tubs, wet bathing suits, wet towels and washcloths), and as a sexually transmitted disease (STD). It is caused by the single-celled protozoan parasite *Trichomonas vaginalis*, Trichomoniasis is primarily an infection of the urogenital tract; the most common site

of infection is the urethra and the vagina in women. It is most common in women and uncircumcised men. For uncircumcised men, the most common site for the infection is the tip of the penis.

Typically, only women experience symptoms associated with *Trichomonas* infection.

Symptoms include:

Vaginitis - itching, burning, and inflammation of the vagina

Cervicitis - inflammation of the cervix

Urethritis - inflammation of the urethra

Green/Yellow, frothy vaginal discharge

Most men with trichomoniasis do not have signs or symptoms; however, some men may temporarily have an irritation inside the penis, mild discharge, or slight burning after urination or ejaculation.

Some women have signs or symptoms of infection which include a frothy, yellow-green vaginal discharge with a strong odor. The infection also may cause discomfort during intercourse and urination, as well as irritation and itching of the female genital area. In rare cases, lower abdominal pain can occur. Symptoms usually appear in women within 5 to 28 days of exposure. [34]

Human papillomavirus (HPV)

Human papillomaviruses (HPVs) are a group of more than 100 related viruses. They are called papillomaviruses because certain types may cause warts, or papillomas, which are benign (noncancerous) tumors. The HPVs that cause the common warts which grow on hands and feet are different from those that cause growths in the throat or genital area. Some types of HPV are associated with certain types of cancer. These are called high-risk, oncogenic, or carcinogenic HPVs. [35] Genital HPV infections are very common and are sexually transmitted. Of the more than 100 types of HPV, more than 30 types can be passed from one person to another through sexual contact. Although HPVs are usually transmitted sexually, doctors cannot say for certain when infection occurred. Most HPV infections occur without any symptoms and go away without any treatment over the course of a few years. However, HPV infection sometimes persists for many years, with or without causing cell abnormalities. This can increase a woman's risk of developing cervical cancer. [36]

Persistent HPV infections are now recognized as the major cause of cervical cancer. In 2007, it was estimated that 11,000 women in the United States would be diagnosed with this type of cancer and nearly 4,000 would die from it. Cervical cancer strikes nearly half a million women each year worldwide, claiming a quarter of a million lives. Studies also suggest that HPVs may play a role in some cancers of the anus, vulva, vagina, and penile cancer (cancer of the penis). [37] The surest way to eliminate risk for genital HPV infection is to refrain from any genital contact with another individual. HPV infection can occur in both male and female genital areas that are covered or protected by a latex condom, as well as in areas that are not covered. Although the degree of protection provided by condoms in preventing HPV infection is unknown, condom use has been associated with a lower rate of cervical cancer. There is currently no medical cure for human papillomavirus infection. It's only the lesions and warts these viruses cause that can be treated. [38]

Some of the symptoms of HPV are: Visible warts in the genital area, including the thighs (Warts can be raised or flat, alone or in groups, small or large, and sometimes they are cauliflower-shaped) and lesions on the cervix and in the genital.

Genital warts

Genital warts, sometimes referred to as condyloma acuminata is a highly contagious sexually transmitted infection caused by some sub-types of human papillomavirus (HPV). It is spread through direct skin-to-skin contact during oral, genital, or anal sex with an infected partner. Genital warts are the most easily recognized sign of genital HPV infection. [39]

Genital warts affect both men and women and can occur at any age. Most patients with genital warts are between the ages of 17-33 years. Genital warts are highly contagious. There is a 60% risk of getting the infection from a single sexual contact with someone who has genital warts.

In children younger than three years, genital warts are thought to be transmitted by nonsexual methods such as direct manual contact. Nevertheless, the presence of genital warts in children should raise the suspicion for sexual abuse. [40]

Genital warts often occur in clusters and can be very tiny or can spread into large masses in the genital or penis area. In women they occur on the outside and inside of the vagina, on the opening (cervix) to the womb (uterus), or around the anus. They are approximately as prevalent in men, but the symptoms may be less obvious. When present, they usually are seen on the tip of the penis. They also may be found on the shaft of the penis, on the scrotum, or around the anus. Rarely, genital warts also can develop in the mouth or throat of a person who has had oral sex with an infected person. [41]

There is no cure for HPV, but there are methods to treat visible warts. Genital warts may disappear without treatment, but sometimes eventually develop a fleshy, small raised growth. There is no way to predict whether they will grow or disappear.[42] Condom usage is not effective against contacting genital warts.

Pelvic inflammatory disease (PID)
Pelvic inflammatory disease (PID) is a serious infection in the upper genital tract/reproductive organs (uterus, fallopian tubes and ovaries) of a female. PID can be sexually transmitted or naturally occurring. It can lead to infertility in women (unable to have children) or life-threatening complications. [43]

If PID goes untreated, it can lead to serious long-term complications, including chronic pelvic pain, ectopic pregnancy (when an embryo begins to develop in the fallopian tube) or infertility. Unfortunately, many women don't know they have PID until permanent damage has been done. [44]

PID develops when bacteria (germs) get into a woman's internal reproductive organs. There are a number of ways this can happen. The internal organs are usually protected by the cervix, which blocks bacteria in the vagina from moving up into the womb. But when the cervix is open (e.g. during menstruation or at ovulation), or if the cervix itself becomes infected, bacteria have a greater chance of getting through and causing infection. Bacteria may also get into the reproductive organs during pelvic surgery or invasive procedures that disrupt the cervix, such as abortion, childbirth or insertion of an IUD (intra-uterine device). Bacteria from severe appendicitis can lead to PID if it spreads to the pelvic tissues, but this is uncommon.[45] It was first thought that IUD can cause PID, but it was later discovered that it is the process of insertion that makes bacteria escape into the uterus. So, it is safer to test a woman for STDs before inserting IUD for her.

Two other sexually transmitted diseases (STDs), chlamydia and gonorrhea, are the most common causes of PID. Other bacteria or germs can also cause PID. If you have an infection in the genital tract and do not get treated right away, it can cause PID. The infection spreads from the cervix into the uterus, fallopian tubes, and ovaries. It can take anywhere from several days to several months after being infected to develop PID. [46]

Although the PID infection itself may be cured, effects of the infection may be permanent. If the initial infection is mostly in the lower tract, after treatment the person may have few difficulties. If the infection is in the fallopian tubes or ovaries, more serious complications are more likely to occur.

Some of the symptoms of PID include: Dull pain or tenderness in the lower abdomen, burning or pain when you urinate (pee) nausea and vomiting, bleeding between menstrual periods, increased or changed vaginal discharge, pain during sex, fever and chills, it is possible for a woman to have PID and be asymptomatic (without symptoms), or have symptoms too mild to notice, for an unknown period of time. [47]

PID can also be misdiagnosed as appendicitis, ectopic pregnancy, ruptured ovarian cysts or other problems.

Fertility may be restored in women affected by PID. Traditionally tuboplastic surgery was the main approach to correct tubal obstruction or adhesion formation; however success rates tended to be very limited. In vitro fertilization (IVF) has been used to bypass tubal problems and has become the main treatment for patients who want to become pregnant. [48]

Conclusion

STDs can lead to serious health problems like cervical cancer and other cancers, liver disease, pelvic inflammatory disease, infertility, pregnancy problems and other complications. [49]

Apart from the risk of "unwanted" pregnancies in premarital sex, STDs can also adversely affect the unborn baby. "STDs can have many of the same consequences for pregnant women as women who are not pregnant. An STD may also cause early labour, cause the water to break early, and cause infection in the uterus after the birth.

Some STDs can be passed from a pregnant woman to the baby before and during the baby's birth. Some STDs, like syphilis, cross the placenta and infect the baby while it is in the uterus. Other STDs, like gonorrhea, chlamydia, hepatitis B, and genital herpes, can be passed from the mother to the baby during delivery as the baby passes through the birth canal. HIV can cross the placenta during pregnancy, and infect the baby during the birth process.

The harmful effects to babies may include low birth weight (less than five pounds), eye infection, pneumonia, infection in the baby's blood, brain damage, lack of coordination in body movements, blindness, deafness, acute hepatitis, meningitis, chronic liver disease, cirrhosis, or stillbirth. Some of these problems can be prevented if the mother receives routine prenatal care, which includes screening tests for STDs starting early in pregnancy and repeated close to delivery, if necessary. Other problems can be treated if the infection is found at birth." [50]

The true solution

The true solution to STDs cannot be found in the usage of condom or science. It is true that science has helped a great deal and that using condom can reduce being infected with some STDs, but using condom cannot prevent all STDs. In situations where it does prevent, the prevention is not foolproof. It can burst, leak or malfunction in any other way. The 'safe sex' propaganda is a scam. The ABC approach is an absurdity. Let's look at it: You just told somebody to abstain or be faithful in marriage, and at the same time, you give him a condom or encourage him to get one in case he considers what you have just told him to be a heap of rubbish? The summary of what young people get from the ABC propaganda is simply put: 'I can have sex if I like, but I should use condom if I am smart". The issue of the fear of God is completely out of the question. I wonder why we don't give young people something to wear in case they feel like jumping in front of a moving train. We could have told them something like: "abstain from jumping before a moving train, but if you can't do without jumping, use a special coat for protection from obvious death." It is possible to jump before a moving train without being killed or sustaining any injury –probably if you missed the train. But because of the possibility of being crushed to death by a moving train, we don't give our young people any alternative to "not to jump". Why can't we do this same thing about premarital sex and stop watching our leaders of tomorrow being slowly crushed to death daily? STD is already a pandemic and we cannot pretend about it.

Sexually Transmitted Diseases

Most of the "safe sex" advocates are only interested in the deception they spread for the money they get from it. They get a lot of government and private company financial aids every year to help keep their businesses running. Some faith-based non-governmental organizations have also compromised the standard of God's word which they are supposed to stand for by preaching the gospel of "safe sex" and distributing condoms to youths and church people! Of course, this compromise entitles them to free funding from donors who won't support them unless they agree to help distribute more condoms.

The true solution is in our returning to the spiritual and moral guidance God, the creator has provided for us. "God knows how we work best and gave us an 'owner's manual' for the human race: the Bible. In it he tells us not to have sex until we are married; not to have sex with anybody other than the one man/one woman to whom we are married; and to stay married the rest of our lives. That's the one and only prescription for safe sex. [51]

Abstinence is rubbish?
For those who will still insist on following their own path, a letter from a lady who suffered a great deal from HPV

may act as a further check. Bear it in mind that HPV can affect areas that are protected by condom and areas that are not protected by condom. This means that the use of condom is not effective in the prevention of HPV in both males and females. HPV also has no cure. This lady wrote this letter to Dr Dobson as a response to Dr Dobson's radio broadcasts on HPV.

"Dear Dr Dobson,

In one of your radio broadcasts you covered the fact that it [HPV] can cause cervical dysplasia leading to cancer of the cervix. Certainly, that's tragic. But it has many other effects that I have not read anything about.

Let me tell you about this disease and what it's done to my life. I'm a twenty-five-year-old college graduate. I've remained single and childless. That singleness is imposed on me by my physical condition. The last four years of my life have been lived with chronic pain, two outpatient surgeries, multiple office biopsies, thousands of dollars in prescriptions and no hope. The effect of this problem is one of severe relentless infection. This condition can be so severe that the pain is almost unbearable. A sexual relationship, or the possibility of marriage, is out of the question.

The isolation is like a knife that cuts my heart out daily. Depression, rage, and hopelessness, and a drastically affected social and religious life are the result. Physicians say they are seeing this condition more commonly. Females are being sentenced to a life of watching others live, marry, and have babies. Please take what I have written to the airwaves.

Thank you for listening, Dr Dobson. This obstacle has been the one that I cannot gain victory over" [52]

8
Questions & Answers

1. I am 12 years old and experiencing changes in my body. They said it is puberty. Please, what is puberty and what changes do I expect in my body?

Yes, what you are experiencing is a stage of growth known as puberty. It is very normal and expected. Puberty is the process of physical changes in a child's body, making his/her body to become an adult body, which is capable of reproduction. Puberty is set in motion by the sex hormones which are testosterone in boys and estrogen in girls. The pituary gland releases special hormones into the body, which triggers the testes to produce testosterone and sperm in boys. Testosterone is the hormone that causes changes in a boy's body, while the sperm is what makes the boy capable of reproduction (becoming a father). In girls, the hormones from the pituary gland triggers the ovaries to produce estrogen, which causes changes in a girl's body, prepare her body to start having her menstrual periods and make her capable of reproduction (becoming a mother). Rapid growth and changes take place in a child's brain, bones, muscle, skin, breasts and reproductive organs. The bodies of boys and girls begin to take different shapes to suit their genders. The boy is transforming into an adult man while the girl is transforming into an adult woman. A girl goes through puberty within the average age of 9-14, while for boys; it is the average age of 10-17. Girls usually begin the process of puberty, 1-2 years before boys.

During puberty, a girl's body goes through the following changes: The first physical sign of the onset of puberty in girls is a 'breast bud'. The breasts start to grow, followed by first signs of hair in the pubic area and armpit. She also starts to increase rapidly in height. The vagina starts to produce a whitish discharge (this is a normal cleansing process). The first menstruation called 'the menarche' follows. The menstruation starts coming at irregular periods for about two years after the menarche. Next to the menarche, ovulation (release of egg cells) begins. Ovulation begins mostly after the menarche. At this stage, the girl is capable of becoming pregnant if sexually active. At the later stages, the body shape changes. The hips widen. Fat tissues increases and are distributed to the breasts, hips, buttocks, thighs, upper arms and the pubis. The hormones also cause body odours, especially in the armpits and a high susceptibility to acne. Some young people worry about the presence of acne. This is a normal situation with people going through puberty. It usually disappears after puberty except in some rare cases.

During puberty, a boy's body goes through the following changes: The first physical sign of the onset of puberty in boys is that the testicles and scrotum begin to enlarge. He starts to increase rapidly in height. The penis starts to grow in length at first, and later, it also starts to increase in width. Hair starts to grow in the pubic area and the armpits. His voice begins to deepen. He experiences his first ejaculation. Facial hair increases on the chin and upper lip. The skin also gets oilier. The body develops muscles and heavier bones especially in the jaw and shoulder. Body odour and acne show presence. The chest also develops hair in some men at the latter stage of puberty.

Puberty begins at various ages between individuals and between populations. Genetic factors and nutrition play important roles in determining the specific age puberty starts for different kids.

2. Why should I save sex for marriage?
There are four major reasons why you should save sex till marriage:

1. God commanded it: It is not a matter of what you and I think, it's a matter of what God thinks and commanded. If you have some respect for God, you will do what He says. God is a God of purpose. He created sex with purpose in mind. Sex is for procreation, pleasure and to build intimacy between a man and a woman as husband and wife. "God also knew that because sex is so powerful in creating intimacy that there must be some constraints on how it was to be used, so He specifically relegated sex to the arena of marriage. The kind of intimacy that God desires between married couples cannot occur between one person and several others; it can only be experienced between one man and one woman. Hence God has specifically said, "Do not commit adultery" (Exodus 20:14), and "Flee sexual immorality" (1 Corinthians 6:18). That is, do not have sex with someone who is not your spouse. Obedience requires that sex be reserved for one's spouse."[53] God sees premarital sex as sexual promiscuity, immorality and fornication.

Questions And Answers

2. You need to show some respect for your future partner by keeping your body for him/her from now. He/she will surely be glad you did. I'm sure you will be glad if your partner does too.

3. You need a healthy body to enjoy your future and your marriage. Premarital sex will expose your body to sexual transmitted diseases (STDs), most of which can maim or kill. Several adults are presently regretting and secretly crying over how they sexually abused their bodies when they were singles because of some consequences they are now battling with.

4. You can get pregnant or become a father when you are not ready for the responsibility. This may greatly distort your future plans. If you opt for abortion, you will be strangulating the life of an unborn baby. That is murder, the guilt of which you may have to carry for a lifetime. It's better to do the right things at the right time.

3. My boy friend said he would leave me unless he has sex with me. I love him and don't want to lose him. What should I do? I am still a virgin.

If your boyfriend would not respect your view and decision to be chaste, then you may not be able to determine whether he really loves you or not. If he threatens to leave you unless he sleeps with you, you can be sure he is most likely going to abandon you once he has his way. There is no fear in love. You should not allow yourself to be stampeded into breaking your decision to delay sex till marriage. You must let him know that you are simply obeying God's instructions. A boy who wants you to disobey God has no regard for God. If the boy really loves you as you love him, he will respect your decision and stop bothering you for sex. So, if he wants to leave, let him leave. There are so many godly guys looking for chaste girls like you to marry. It is not enough for you to love a boy; the boy must also love and respect you before you can take him serious for whatever he tells you.

4. I and my boyfriend had slept together several times before now. Now that I have realized the negative effects and consequences of premarital sex, I told him we should stop having sex until we are married, but he refused. He is threatening to date another person. What should I do, as I don't desire to lose him?

Questions And Answers

No matter how far you have gone on a wrong road, a u-turn is permitted. It's good you've realized your wrong ways and have decided to make a u-turn. Take your time to explain to him why you've arrived at this new decision. You can share the same materials and Bible passages you read or give him the tape or compact disk of the message you listened to. Try to take him through the process you went through before you arrived at your new decision and see if he can also catch up with you.

If he fails to see reason with you, make sure you maintain your stand and let him see the seriousness of your decision. If he loves you enough, he will respect your feelings. In case he opts to date somebody else, that means he was only using you to fulfil his sexual desires. He never really loved you from his heart. Another thing you should consider is that if he is somebody who cannot exercise control over his sexual passion, then you can't really tell if you are the only girl in his life, or that he will be faithful to you if you get married to him. Let him know your stand and make up his mind. If he leaves, somebody else will come.

5. My own question is slightly different from the above. My own problem is that it is this boy that broke my

virginity. I have made up my mind that whosoever breaks my virginity is the person I will marry. Now, he wants to leave unless I allow him to continue to have sex with me. I have repented of my sins and have promised God to henceforth delay sex till marriage. I am caught between two opinions. Please what do you advise?

I can understand your feelings, but I still advise you maintain your stand. That he broke your virginity is not a proof that he is the best person for you. It is unfortunate that you did not know the right thing to do about your sexuality on time. Nevertheless, it is not too late as you have decided to amend your ways now. Remember your promise to God. It is better to please God rather than man. God will touch his heart to understand with you if he is really the man for you. Otherwise, if he chooses to leave because you won't agree to have premarital sex with him, let him go. You have chosen to honour God with your body. God will also honour you, and you will have no regrets about your decision for purity and righteousness. You should also know that marriage is much more than having sex. You are not a sex-machine or sex-toy for your boyfriend. He should start learning how to treat you as a person and respect your views.

6. My friends said I am not yet a man until I prove myself in bed with a girl. Are they right?

They are dead wrong! You are the real man because you can exercise control over your sexual desires. It takes real men to accomplish that feat. Falling head-over-heels after women is for the weak that are not in control of their lives, but are being pushed around by their sexual passions and feelings. They are guys who are unable to make up their minds because they really don't know what they want. So, they keep rising and falling into errors every day. You don't have to commit the sin of fornication to show that you are a man. Fornication only proves that you are a sinner, wallowing in the mire of sin like a pig. If you can hold up your head in this corrupt and perverse generation, you are the real man. A thumb up for you!

7. My friends said I am not in their class because I am still a virgin. I am eighteen years old. They call me names like 'ignorant', 'unexposed' and 'inexperienced'. I feel rejected, but how can I convince them of my stand?

Let your friends know that it is your choice and decision to remain chaste. Everybody has a choice. Don't feel rejected; your friends really need you to explain the necessity of chastity to them. Explain to them that chastity is a commandment from God. To be at peace with God, we must obey His commandments. Let them know that chastity will help your future marriage and shield you from unnecessary distractions from pursuing your future plans. They may laugh at you, but for sure in their hearts, they admire you and wish they are like you.

Let them know they are the ignorant ones, because if they know what you know, they will live differently. Let them know it is very foolish of them to keep exposing themselves to the dangers of a sinful life, STDs and a possibility of untimely death all because of a momentary pleasure which they can always enjoy to its fullest at the right time, when they get married. Let them know that chastity is the true experience of peace.

Do your best to tell your friends about the blessing and freedom of being chaste. Encourage them to also have a change of heart. Nevertheless, if they won't listen to you, friendship is also by choice. You may have to reduce your contacts with such people.

8. Will I fall sick if I don't have sex?

The opposite is the truth. You are very likely going to fall sick and probably die if you sleep around. Even if you use condom, you are still at risk. Condom cannot protect you from every sexually transmitted disease. It's a pity that this truth had been kept away from people for a long time. The failure rate of condom is also very high. Why hang your life in the balance? Living a life of chastity does not expose you to any form of sickness or disease. You cannot fall sick as a result of not having sex. When Satan wants to bind a man, he sells him a lie. Don't buy this lie. Stay free.

9. My girlfriend wants me to have sex with her, but my conscience says no. Is she the right girl for me?
I doubt very much if she is the right girl for you. If she wants sex so desperately, she can always get it elsewhere. You must tread softly with such a girl. Take time to educate her for her to see why you should both delay having sex until marriage. If after that, she still wants to have sex, let her go. She is not the girl for you.

10. My parents don't see anything wrong in premarital sex. They said I should only be careful and play safe. Are they right?

Parents are not usually right 100 percent of the time, but I believe they are sincere. What you need to do is to engage them in discussions on chastity and abstinence. I am sure they will agree with your stand. They might have told you to play safe because they were not sure of what you may do. You know, parents sometimes are also battling with temptations even as married people. Parents who find it difficult to be sexually faithful may consider it useless advising their children to be chaste. They feel it is impossible. The truth is that it is possible to abstain from sex before marriage and be faithful to spouse in marriage.

11. My lecturer is threatening me with failure in his course unless I sleep with him. What should I do? I don't want to fail.

It is highly disturbing these days to realize that some of those whom the society had invested with the responsibility of nurturing our children through education are the very ones corrupting them. If your lecturer asks you for sex and you are not interested in his advances, refuse him. Let him know your stand as a Christian and that fornication is a sin against God and your future spouse. If he refuses to bulge, take his matter to God in prayers. You can ask other trusted brethren in your church/fellowship to join you in prayer over the matter. God answers prayers. You can ask God to touch his heart and cause a change or, ask God to confuse his mind until he enters into trouble. Some lecturers had been prayed out of their jobs this way because they will not allow daughters of Zion to rest.

Something else you can do is to report him to trusted Christian lecturers who can speak to him on your behalf. When I was an undergraduate, one of our Christian lecturers used to do this on behalf of some of our sisters in the fellowship and it really did helped.

On your own side, make sure you prepare very well for his exam such that it will be hard for him to fail you.

As a last resort, if he ends up failing you, you can protest your marks to the school's authorities. Pray and seek God's leading before taking any of these steps. Sometimes, those threats may be empty threats just to coerce you into sleeping with him. God may also touch his heart and he will not fail you.

12. How else can I keep myself in school since my parents are poor? What other alternatives do I have to sleeping

with rich men? I am an undergraduate and twenty-one years old.

There are so many things you can do to raise money as an undergraduate instead of prostituting your body in case your parents can't be financially responsible for you.

i. You can look for something to sell. I know someone who paid her way through her university education by selling food stuffs to her fellow students. She sold from her room. She also paid for her siblings' school fees from her business.

ii. You can look for a part time job on the campus. A student once applied to her school and was employed as a cleaner to pay her way through.

iii. You can study hard to win scholarships.

iv. You can use your holiday time to work and save for your school fees.

v. You can talk to other relatives of yours. Who knows, somebody might want to help.

vi. You can look for a permanent job and go to school as a part time student.

vii. If you live in a developed country, you can apply for a student loan to take care of your school fees.

Once you look at other options, you will discover that prostitution is not the only option you have. You should rather, remove prostitution from the list of things you can do to raise funds for your education. You need a healthy body to enjoy the benefits of your education after graduation. I am positive that very soon in the developing countries; it will also be possible for students to access loans for their education.

13. Is it really possible to do without sex until marriage?
It is possible. It only requires a decision and strong determination to be chaste. You need to choose to be righteous. Temptations will come, but God is able to help you overcome those temptations. Take precautions against putting yourself in situations where it may be difficult for you to resist temptations. Don't feed on garbage like pornography or illicit novels and films. Make up your mind to live chaste and God will help you.

14. Is sex not just a fulfilling of natural appetites like eating?

Yes, sexual urge is natural, but not like hunger pang. Having sex is not the same thing like eating food. Sex should be an expression of love and intimacy between husband and wife. Eating food does not involve intimacy with another person. Those who equate having sex to eating food usually hop from bed to bed since they need to taste different kinds of food. This is a satanic deception to bind men and women with the spirit of immorality.

15. I didn't hear this earlier! I should have kept my virginity. What can I do now?

It's o.k. that you now know the importance of sexual purity. You cannot undo the past. What has happened has happened. There is nothing you can really do about that.

What you can do now is to acknowledge your errors of the past as sin before God and ask God to forgive you. God will surely cleanse you with the shed blood of His son. Also go before the lord in prayers and break every covenant between you and your past sexual partners.

Be pure from now on. Don't return into the mire of sexual immorality. God will help you as you make up your mind to live pure.

Lastly, be truthful to your future life partner. Don't lie to him about your past. Don't tell him you are a virgin when you know you are not. "Be honest with anyone who is a "potential spouse" - don't wait till your wedding night to discuss your sexual past. Some intimacy problems may be averted if you address them early on."[54]

16. I already lost my virginity, am I still valuable?

Your value in life is not attached to your virginity status. It has to do with how you carry yourself. It is the value you put on yourself that people will put on you. Everybody has a past. Put your past behind you and move on in life. When you enter into a relationship, don't lie about your virginity status. If a man cannot love you and marry you the way you are, he is not worthy of you. You can still be happily married and be all that God ordained you to be if you will not look down on yourself. Forgive yourself, ask for God's forgiveness and live a life of chastity from now on. You are still a jewel of inestimable value!

17. What negative effect can premarital sex have on ones marriage?

Premarital sex can have a lot of negative effects on ones marriage in so many ways:

i. The first thing premarital sex robs you of in marriage is the excitement and anticipation of your first night together as husband and wife. If you've been sleeping together before marriage, you miss this excitement and anticipation. You start your marriage on a zero speed. Nothing is really new except that you now have a marriage certificate. You already stole the 'honey' in your 'moon'.

ii. Premarital sex gives you a basis for comparison. If you have slept with other people other than your marriage partner, you may end up thinking somebody else could do it better than your spouse. This kind of feeling, if not intentionally curtailed, may lead to comparison syndrome or unfaithfulness in marriage.

iii. Your marriage partner runs the risk of carrying the infections you might have contacted from other people through sex.

iv. Premarital sex could have led to pregnancies and abortions in the past, which might make it difficult or impossible to bear children in marriage.

v. If your spouse had kept the law of chastity before marriage, he/she may feel you really do not love and respect him/her enough by not preserving yourself for him/her. This may negatively affect your intimacy.

vi. Don't forget, premarital sex is a sin against God.

There could be other negative effects of premarital sex on marriage. That is why it pays to obey God's commandments.

18. Why do I need to keep myself pure when I am not sure my future partner will do the same?

Since you do not yet know your future partner, how are you also sure your future partner will not keep himself or herself pure? Nevertheless, the number one reason why you should keep yourself pure is not really because of your future partner. The first reason why you should live pure is because God commanded it. If you eventually found out that your future partner did not obey God's commandment in this area, let it be between him and God.

19. If we delay sex till marriage, what happens if we discover after marriage that we are not sexually compatible?

How do we 'gauge' sexual compatibility? If you need to try a couple of partners to see which one is sexier than the rest, you are already in for trouble. While you thought you've found your most sexually compatible partner, you may just try one more person and discover you are yet to reach your destination. The search for the most sexually compatible partner is endless. No matter how pretty or handsome your partner is, you will soon meet someone more handsome or prettier. Do you dump your partner in pursuit of the prettier you just discovered?

The truth is that the concept of sexual compatibility does not exist if you have only one sexual partner. You really don't have a basis for comparison. Sex is the same. It is an illusion to start looking for a 'sexually compatible' partner. Most people only give this reason to satisfy their sexual lust and desires before marriage. Anybody who wishes to disobey God can always find a reason.

Married couples can always improve on their sexual life through reading, counselling, attending marriage seminars and discoveries of themselves through practice. Successful marriage is much more than having sex. Anybody who uses sexual prowess to select a partner may easily fall into the hands of a prostitute whom only he/she cannot satisfy.

20. What are Sexually Transmitted Diseases (STDs)?

STDs are diseases that are sexually transferable from person to person. Some STDs are incurable and can lead to excruciating pain, liver failure, skin rashes, infertility and even death. "It is said that 65 percent of all STDs occur among persons less than twenty-five years of age."[55] "There is only one safe way to remain healthy in the midst of a sexual revolution. It is to abstain from intercourse until marriage, and then wed and be faithful to an uninfected partner." [56]

21. What do experts think about HIV and condoms?

"At the national Conference on HIV in 1991, some 800 sexologists were asked to raise their hand if they would trust a condom to protect them during intercourse with a known HIV-infected person. Not one of them did."[57]

22. Is it not right to encourage safe sex through the use of condom since kids are going to have sex anyhow?

The Beauty Of Virginity

Let me answer this question in the very words of Rush Limbaugh:

"Condom distribution sanctions, even encourages, sexual activity, which in teen years tends to be promiscuous and relegates to secondary status the most important lesson to be taught: abstinence. An analysis of the entire condom distribution logic also provides a glimpse into just what is wrong with public education today.

Advocates of condom distribution say that kids are going to have sex, that try as we might we can't stop them. Therefore they need protection, hence, condoms. Well, hold on a minute. Just whose notion is it that 'kids are going to do it anyway, you can't stop them?' Why limit the application of that brilliant logic to sexual activity? Let's just admit that kids are going to do drugs and distribute safe, untainted drugs every morning in homeroom. Kids are going to smoke too; we can't stop them, so let's provide packs of low-tar cigarettes to the students for their after-sex smoke. Kids are going to get guns and shoot them; you can't stop them, so let's make sure that teachers have bulletproof vests. I mean, come on! If we are really concerned about safe sex, why stop at condoms? Let's convert study halls to Safe Sex Centers where students can go to actually have sex on nice double beds with clean sheets under the watchful and approving eye of the school nurse, who will be on hand to demonstrate, along with the principal, just how to use a condom. Or even better: If kids are going to have sex, let's put disease-free hookers in these Safe Sex Centers. Hey, if safe sex is the objective, why compromise our standards?

Well, here's what's wrong. There have always been consequences to having sex. Always. Now, however, some of these consequences are severe: debilitating venereal diseases and AIDS. You can now die from having sex. It is that simple. If you look, the vast majority of adults in America have made adjustments in their sexual behavior in order to protect themselves from some of the dire consequences floating around out there. For the most part, the sexual revolution of the sixties is over, a miserable failure. Free love and rampant one-night stands are tougher to come by because people are aware of the risks. In short, we have modified our behavior. Now, would someone tell me what is so difficult about sharing this knowledge and experience with kids? The same stakes are involved. Isn't that our responsibility, for crying out loud, to teach them what's best for them? If we adults aren't responding to these new dangers by having condom-protected sex anytime, anywhere, why should such folly be taught to our kids?

Doesn't it make sense to be honest with kids and tell them the best thing they can do to avoid AIDS or any of the other undesirable consequences is to abstain from sexual intercourse? It is the best way - in fact, is it the only surefire way - to guard against sexual transmission of AIDS, pregnancy, and venereal diseases. What's so terrible about saying so?"[58]

23. If I am careful enough, can't I avoid pregnancy and STDs?

Yes, you can be lucky sometimes, but the truth is that you cannot be careful enough every time. Accidents do happen. Are you really ready to trade a few moments of pleasure for the rigors of caring for an unwanted pregnancy and a life time of pain, grief and untimely death?

24. Can I start a relationship without sex?

Yes, you can start a relationship without sex. You can also keep a relationship till you tie the knot without sex. In fact, that is what you should do. The purpose of having a relationship should not be for sex, but for intimacy. If the main reason why you need a relationship is for sex, then you don't need a relationship. What you need is a prostitute. Only count the cost before you plunge your head into the sea. There might be cobras and sharks waiting to eat you up. The purpose of starting a relationship is to develop intimacy with someone of the opposite sex with the view of seeing if the relationship can lead into marriage. Sex before marriage is promiscuity.

25. "Is it okay to have sex if you're totally in love with each other, and you're totally certain that you're going to marry each other and spend the rest of your lives together (especially if you're engaged to be married)? What if you're over 30 (or 40), or what if you had previously been married before? Is premarital sex okay at that point?"

"Notice that after you are married, then sex is appropriate between you and your spouse. But before you are married it is still premarital sex (fornication). So if premarital sex is a sin, then it is a sin up until the moment you are married. The New Testament never says that if you're totally in love with each other and you're committed to each other and you're certain that you will get married and spend the rest of your lives together, then premarital sex is okay. The New Testament also never says that premarital sex is okay if you're over a certain age limit, or if you had previously been married before, or anything like that. Sorry, but there are no "loopholes"!

Also, consider that there are many people, who were engaged to be married, and who expected to spend the rest of their lives together, but then they broke up. Some of them gave their virginity to each other because they were certain that they were going to get married, and they ended up regretting that they gave up their virginity to the wrong person. Life is full of uncertainties, and you're not married until you're married!"[59]

26. How far can we go in having romance as unmarried couples?

Unmarried couples are not supposed to be having romance. "It is human nature to want to know how far we can go without "crossing the line," but remember what the New Testament says:

1 Corinthians 6:18: *"Flee from sexual immorality."*
In the above passage we are told to run away from sexual immorality. Therefore, the best thing to do is not to get

anywhere near "crossing the line." Our analytical minds want to know if it is safe for us to fondle and touch each other sexually (even fully clothed), or to have oral sex instead of intercourse, or to see each other naked, etc., but notice that those are not the attitudes that the Bible describes. All of those things will increase our desire and temptation to have sex, but the Bible says to run away from those temptations. Therefore, it's best to avoid any situations which will cause sexual temptation, such as touching each other sexually, being naked (or near naked) with each other, or sometimes even just being alone together. This can sometimes be difficult to do when our emotions (and hormones) are flying high for that special person, but try to keep in mind that when we follow God's plan then everything always works out for the best, in amazing ways!"[60]

27. Is it o.k. to be a virgin at 16?

It is very o.k. not only to be a virgin at 16, but to be a virgin till whatever age you get married. There is nothing like age limit in keeping your virginity. Keep living responsibly. God will surely reward you.

28. What is fornication?

Fornication is voluntary sexual intercourse between a man and a woman who are not married to each other. So many passages in the Bible warn Christians against indulging in fornication and any other sexual immorality.

29. How can I select my marriage partner?
Next in importance to your salvation is the choice of your marriage partner. A careless or wrong choice can lead to a life of woes and mystery.

i. A believer should seek to marry a fellow believer. Do not be unequally yoked together with unbelievers (II Cor. 6:14-15). A house divided against itself cannot stand (Matt. 12:25).

ii. Be led and guided by God. A Christian should be able to hear from God. Don't just pray (speaking to God), also listen to what God has to tell you.

iii. Do not be led by your emotions or infatuation. Don't be carried away with material things or appearance. Choose a marriage partner on the basis of character, not appearance.

iv. Choose a partner who loves God and is committed to the things of God. The fear of God alone contributes immensely to having a successful marriage.

v. Never marry anyone on the basis that they'll change after marriage.

vi. Seek for marital counselling from your pastor or qualified marriage counsellor.

30. Is sex bad?

Sex is good, but can be misused. Sex is only right and good in marriage. Outside the confines of marriage, it brings dire consequences that can be highly regrettable. Sex was created by God for the purposes of pleasure, procreation and intimacy within the confines of marriage. So, sex is like a double-edged sword. Good if handles properly, dangerous and hurtful if mishandled.

31. I am a virgin, but I dream of having sex and getting married in my dream. Am I still a virgin?

If you see yourself having sex and getting married in your dream, that is a spiritual problem. It has nothing to do with your virginity. Those who had lost their virginity also do have such problems. What you need is a deliverance ministration to break the demonic powers of darkness coming to defile you in your dream. These forces of darkness are referred to as spirit husbands/wives. They are anti-productivity and anti-marriage spirits. Once their power is broken over your life in prayers, those useless dreams will stop.

If you are yet to have a physical sexual relationship with anybody, you are still a virgin. Those spirit husbands/wives cannot break your physical virginity. You need a physical human being to do that. So, you are still a virgin, but you need deliverance ministrations.

32. What truly is safe sex?

The true 'safe sex' is abstinence before marriage and faithfulness in marriage. Any other form of 'safe sex' propaganda is deception. Who says you can't abstain or be faithful in marriage? If you believe you can do all things through Christ who strengthens you, then you can. Stop buying into the lie that you can't. If it is possible for just one person in your generation to abstain or be faithful in marriage, then you too can. Please be rightly informed that so many people in your neighbourhood are abstaining before marriage and staying faithful to their spouse in marriage.

Incredibly, some young people are still getting married as virgins. You too can do it!

33. What is the ABC approach to safe sex?

The ABC approach to 'safe sex' is: A -abstinence, B -be faithful and C -use condom. This is the very approach some of us are against. I will rather go for 'A' and 'B' because 'C' makes a mess of the whole effort. It is true that condom can prevent some STDs, but what happens to the STDs it can't prevent like, genital warts, the dreaded human papillomavirus (HPV) and pelvic inflammatory disease (PID)? What also happens when there are condom accidents? At the end of the day, it's like nothing concrete is being done to prevent anything. Only the lucky ones escape from contacting STDs. Who cares for the others who are still at risk while wearing the condom or the 'fast' ones who have discovered that wearing condom is a hindrance to true enjoyment of sex, and have decided to do away with the obstacle? It is only when we emphasize abstinence and sexual faithfulness in marriage, without deflating the message with dashing out condoms that we can make any real progress in the prevention of STDs.

34. Sometimes, the sexual urge grips me and I feel like having sex. In view of the fact that I don't want to continue in my old sinful way, what should I do at such times of temptation?

It is good you have made up your mind not to continue in your old sinful way. That is the very first thing you need to do. Once your mind is made up for a clean life-style, the rest is simple. Anytime you feel the urge or feel tempted, quickly remind yourself of your decision. Say to yourself; 'that is in the past'. Take your focus away from whatever is the source of that temptation. If nothing really prompted the feeling, i.e. if you just woke up and you discover your body is filled with passion, quickly occupy yourself with something else. You can take your Bible to meditate on God's word or go on your knees to pray. You may also get up from the bed and go find something to do. Don't start meditating and fantasizing on your feeling.

Also remember you are in control of what you use your body to do. The control center of your being is your mind. Once promiscuity is no longer in your mind, it can't find a way into your body. The mind is so important in the fight for morality. Even Satan CANNOT force you to do whatever you have made up your mind not to do. Satan does not have such powers. If Satan can force anybody, he would have forced everybody. It's the same way God does not force anybody to live righteous. If God does forces people to be righteous, there would be no sinner on earth. So, you must know that you are in charge of how you use your body. Satan wants you to believe in your mind that you can't survive a minute without premarital sex or sexual unfaithfulness in marriage. He (Satan) is so much focused on your mind because he knows that if he can defeat you in your mind, you are already defeated. Satan is using so many medium to confuse people's mind about their God-given ability to say no to sin through music, television, internet, pornography, etc.

To have sexual urges is natural. It shows that your reproductive system is alive. That does not mean you have to go beyond limits to commit sin. Sometimes, you pass by something that doesn't belong to you and you feel like stealing. Somehow, you tell yourself that you are not a thief and walk pass the item. You don't want to commit the sin/offence of stealing. You also don't want to risk the possibility of being caught (which is very real) and the shame of being labelled a thief. The same way, you can overcome the temptation to commit fornication or adultery by processing the thought in your mind correctly. Once the temptation can't sail through successfully in your mind, you overcome it.

Temptations are common. You are not the only one being tempted. Several other people are also being tempted and they are not falling to the temptations. God does not allow us to be tempted above what we can handle. God also provides a way of escape out of every temptation. It is however our duties to locate the way of escape God has provided and take advantage of it. You can meditate on this scripture: "There hath no temptation taken you but such as is common to man: but God is faithful, who will not suffer you to be tempted above that ye are able; but will with the temptation also make a way to escape, that ye may be able to bear it" (1 Cor. 10:13).

35. I believe God has forgiven me my past, but why do I still feel guilty each time I remember the things I did in the past?

If you have repented of your sins and accepted Jesus Christ as your lord and saviour, God has forgiven you your sins. Satan is the accuser of brethren. He (Satan) likes to make believers (especially new believers) feel they are not yet forgiven or that they cannot be forgiven so that they can continue in their past sins. The only weapon you can use to conquer the accusations of Satan is the word of God. I John 1:7 says : *"but if we walk in the light as He Himself is in the light, we have fellowship with one another, and the blood of Jesus His Son cleanses us from all sin"* (NASB). Also see: I John 2:1-2, I Cor. 6:11, Eph. 1:7, Heb. 9:14. You need to keep assuring yourself with God's word that you have been forgiven. When Satan hears you quote scriptures, he flees.

You also need to forgive yourself. It's true you made mistakes in the past, but you cannot undo the past. Now that you know better, turn a new leaf and forget whatever happened in the past. Don't judge yourself with your past. You still have a great future to fulfill. Forgive yourself and keep walking in the light of God's word. God has surely forgiven you.

36. How can I break my addiction to pornography?

If you are addicted to pornography, you need your heart to be blood washed. The first thing you need to do is to be born again. Sin has spiritual powers that only the blood of Jesus can break. When you are addicted to substances or acts of immoralities, you are already under a controlling power that is stronger than you. You need the help of a stronger power to help you break the addiction. Only Jesus Christ can deliver you from the power of sin because he conquered sin and death for us.

You also need to make up your mind to live a new life. You have to make adjustments in your life to reflect your new life-style. You have to take a bold step to confirm your change of heart. You can do this by detaching yourself from whatever connected you to pornography through burning all your pornography materials and refraining from any activity or friendship that can expose you further to pornography. Don't ever log on to porn sites again. You can install a filter on your computer.

Guide your heart with all diligence. Take care of your mind by renewing your mind with God's word. As you consistently study God's word, you will be gaining victory over whatever addiction you desire to break in your life.

You can also talk to your pastor about it and seek for counselling and prayers. There are Christian websites where you can have access to materials that can assist you. Search for such sites and fellowship with others who are in the same boat with you.

No matter what, make up your mind to live responsibly and never give in to temptations to return to your old ways. God will help you when your mind is made up to follow His way.

37. Were some people created by God to be homosexuals and lesbians?

God never created anybody for same sex marriage. God created the first human beings as male and female. Adam was a man while Eve was a woman. God joined them together in marriage and blessed them to have dominion, multiply and replenish the earth.

Homosexuality and lesbianism are forms of sexual perversion, also referred to as sodomy. God destroyed Sodom and Gomorrah with fire because of this iniquity. The word of God is very explicit on this topic:

"You shall not lie with a male as one lies with a female; it is an abomination" (Lev 18:22),

"If there is a man who lies with a male as those who lie with a woman, both of them have committed a detestable act; they shall surely be put to death. Their bloodguiltiness is upon them" (Lev 20:13),

"For this reason God gave them over to degrading passions; for their women exchanged the natural function for that which is unnatural, and in the same way also the men abandoned the natural function of the woman and burned in their desire toward one another, men with men committing indecent acts and receiving in their own persons the due penalty of their error" (Romans 1:26-27)

The problem with homosexuals and lesbians is a problem of sexual identity. Identity problems can be a confused self perception which most times are also demonic in nature. People with identity problems need help and prayers. It is not a normal thing to be a homosexual or a lesbian.

38. I just confirmed that I am pregnant. I am not yet ready for marriage. What should I do?

If you confirm that you are pregnant when you are not yet ready for the responsibilities of marriage and motherhood, then you have a big decision to make. It is unfortunate that you didn't wait for the right time, but that does not mean end of the road for you. You can still fulfil your plans, but you'll have to attend to your present situation now and plan to continue your studies or whatever you are presently doing later on.

It is bad enough that you are pregnant at this time, but it will be worse if you attempt to terminate the pregnancy. The baby in your womb has a right to live. Killing the unborn is murder before God. Abortion can also result into infections that may lead to infertility for you in the future. Some also die while trying to abort. You must weigh the implications very well and know that God is against your taking a human life.

If you or the father can't raise the baby and there is nobody to help you raise the baby among your parents or relatives, you can give the baby up for adoption. That is still better than killing your baby. God will strengthen and comfort you as you go through this period of trial in your life.

39. Is it right to masturbate?
Masturbation is the self stimulation of one's own genitals to achieve sexual arousal and orgasm. The stimulation is

usually done manually by hand or with the aid of sex machines such as a vibrator.

There are divergent views on the rightness or wrongness of masturbation. Many Christians believe it is right and healthy to masturbate while many believe it is a sin.

The Bible did not mention anything directly about masturbation, but many believe it is an act of immorality and gratification of the lust of the flesh. It is said that a majority of males and over 50 percent of females indulge in masturbation.

Most young people naturally discover masturbation through exploration of parts of their body. A few others learn it through pornography or group of friends. As much as I agree that most young people naturally stumble on masturbation, I don't believe we should encourage them to continue to indulge in it.

Masturbation usually becomes obsessive and difficult to break as a habit if people see nothing wrong in it. Masturbation is also highly linked to pornography and lust (sexual fantasy). Pornography is 100 percent wrong and lust is clearly a sin. Jesus said in Matthew 5:28 that anyone who looks on a woman lustfully has committed adultery with her already in his heart. The bad effect of masturbation is clearly seen when the habit follows a man/woman into adulthood and marriage. It then becomes a substitute for healthy sexual relationship between husband and wife. This will make couples to start defrauding each other since they can achieve sexual pleasure and climax without the other partner. Married people who are addicted to masturbation are also known not to be easily satisfied by their spouses. Some males even get to the extent that they can no more maintain erection if they want to have sex with their wife unless they masturbate first. This I believe is highly unhealthy.

So, in my own opinion, I believe it is not the right thing to indulge in. Young people will definitely struggle with it, but adults should not even be found near it at all.

40. I have never had sex in my life, yet I discovered that my hymen is broken. What do you think is responsible for this? What do I tell my future spouse?
Apart from sexual intercourse, rigorous sport or the insertion of tampon can cause the hymen to break. However, if any

of these happened, you will know, because you will see blood. If indeed, you did not know when the hymen got broken and cannot remember seeing blood at anytime, there may be a possibility of your having suffered sexual abuse as a baby. When your future spouse arrives, tell him all that you know. Just tell him the truth as it is. I believe you are still a virgin since you never had sex with anyone.

41. I had sex just only once and lost my virginity. Can my virginity be restored if I do not have sex again before marriage? If yes, can I still make my future spouse believe that I am a virgin?

It takes your first sexual intercourse to break your virginity. If it's only once in your lifetime you had sex, you already broke your virginity. Virginity, once broken cannot be naturally restored. Some women go to the extent of faking it with hymenorraphy, which is a surgical repair of the broken hymen. "Pieces of the hymen are sown back with a gelatin capsule containing a blood like substance which breaks and makes it look like blood during the faked 'first' sexual experience."[61] This is nothing but deception. What if somehow, your spouse still got a wind of what actually transpired? Genuine love does not grow in an atmosphere of deception. So, since virginity, once broken cannot be restored, the question of making your future spouse believe that you are a virgin does not arise. Tell your future spouse the truth. Let him know you've had sex just once. Lying to your spouse about your virginity status will have negative effects on your marriage. Once your spouse discovers the truth, it will adversely affect 'intimacy' and 'trust' in your marriage. These are some pillars of a successful marriage you cannot do without.

That you lost your virginity is not the end of the world. What is important is that you start keeping your body for your future spouse from now on. I am sure your future spouse will appreciate you for keeping yourself from now.

42. It is easy for a man to know if his wife is truly a virgin but difficult for a woman to determine if her husband is truly a virgin. How can a woman determine her husband's virginity status?

Just like you have observed it's easier for a man to discover the 'truth' on their first night as husband and wife than for a woman to discover the 'truth'. There is no other way for a woman to determine the virginity status of her husband other than to rely on her husband's testimony. But I must add here that men are not known to be shy or secretive about their sexual past. Men hardly lie about their virginity status. This is because men and women see sex from two different perspectives.

43. My In-laws-to-be want me pregnant before they can consent to our marriage. They claim they have a reason for their demand. Since this is contrary to God's commandments, what should I do?

Thanks for the question, but you did not tell us your fiancé's position on this matter. Is he taking sides with his parents or standing by your side and God's word? If he is a Christian like you, he should naturally stand on God's word like you are doing. Let him be the one to handle his parents. If he succumbs to the dictates of his parents on this issue, that should be a signal to you that he may not run his family on godly principles. Your In-laws' reason or tradition does not matter since the word of God is very clear on the issue of premarital sex.

I advise you to stand by God's word. Don't agree to build your home on the foundation of human tradition. Human tradition will fail, but God's word abides forever.

44. Why is it that women suffer more frequently and more serious complications from STDs than men?

Some of the reasons are:

1. The opening of the female organ is wider than the opening of the male organ. This makes it easier for women to be more susceptible to infections than men.

2. After sex, the man washes himself and goes his way, but the woman is still carrying whatever she collected from the man around for hours after the intercourse. So, the man may escape some infections from the woman, while it's difficult for the woman to escape infections from the man.

3. Pelvic Inflammatory Disease (PID) is a female disease. The most common causes of PID are chlamydia and gonorrhea infections, which infect both males and females. In females however, these infections may be without symptoms and not be treated, giving the bacteria ample time to move into the upper genital tract/reproductive organs (uterus, fallopian tubes and ovaries) thereby causing severe and permanent damages, which may lead to infertility or other life-threatening complications.

45. What does it mean to be sexually assaulted or raped? How can a girl avoid being raped?

Sexual assault/abuse is any type of sexual activity that you do not consent to, including: inappropriate touching, vaginal, anal, or oral penetration, sexual intercourse that you say no to, rape, attempted rape, child molestation, etc.

"Sexual assault can be verbal, visual, or anything that forces a person to join in unwanted sexual contact or attention. Examples of this are voyeurism (when someone watches private sexual acts), exhibitionism (when someone exposes him/herself in public), incest (sexual contact between family members), and sexual harassment. It can happen in different situations, by a stranger in an isolated place, on a date, or in the home by someone you know."[62]

"Rape is a common form of sexual assault. It is committed in many situations - on a date, by a friend or an acquaintance, or when you think you are alone. Educate yourself on "date rape" drugs. They can be slipped into a drink when a victim is not looking. Never leave your drink unattended - no matter where you are. Try to always be aware of your surroundings. Date rape drugs make a person unable to resist assault and can cause memory loss so the victim doesn't know what happened."[63]

If you've been sexually assaulted or raped, don't hide what happened. It's not your fault that somebody took advantage of you and forced you. Call a friend or family member you trust and ask for assistance. Feelings of shame, guilt, fear, and shock are normal. It is important to get assistance from a trusted person or professional. Do not clean up yourself. Do not wash any part of your body. Go straight to the police station to report and let them take you to the hospital for tests for STDs, treatment and evidence documentation. Be sure to press charges against your abductor(s) in a court of law. You have the right to do so without spending a dime. A girl can protect herself from being sexually assaulted or raped by following these steps:

- Don't walk in lonely places all by yourself.
- Don't walk late at night.
- Don't do drugs or alcohol.
- Trust your instincts. If you feel uncomfortable in your surroundings, leave.
- Avoid being behind locked doors with a lover.

- Don't move with bad groups or wayward friends. They may set you up.
- Watch out for unwanted visitors. Know who's on the other side of the door before you   open it.
- Dress moderately. Don't be provocative in your dressing.

46. Why do I have wet sleeps? Is anything wrong about it?

A wet sleep is an ejaculation of semen experienced by a male during sleep. It is also known as nocturnal emission, a spontaneous orgasm, or simply an orgasm during sleep. Wet sleeps are most common during teenage and early adult years. However, wet sleeps may happen any time during or after puberty. Wet sleep is caused by a 'build up' of semen over time in the body. Since nocturnal emission is involuntary, there is nothing wrong about it. However, if it occurs as a result of having sex in dream, that is a spiritual problem with spirit wife/husband. Such a fellow will have to undergo deliverance ministration to break the power of the spirit husband/wife.

Please, if you have further questions or wish to relate an experience, visit: www.remioluyale.com and leave your questions/comments or simply send a mail to: bovirginity@remioluyale.com. Thank you.

9
Parental Guidance

Parents, here we are. It is our responsibility to guide our children through until they are ready to go and form their own homes. Quality time is highly needed to spend with children in order to effectively affect their lives positively and provide answers to their questions.

In counselling children about sex, parents should do their best to educate so that they can't just be easily swept off their feet through misinformation from their peers and the morally retarded modern society.

Parents should be honest and truthful when dealing with their children. They should present both or all sides of the issue and encourage them to choose rightly. Children should be guided in love. The use of coercion on the subject of love will make children withdraw and close up their minds to their parents. This can be very dangerous as parents will be ignorant of what their children are going through or are doing.

Let them know there is a future before them that they need to pursue with moral discipline. Every child can determine his/her destiny through how he/she relates to sex.

Share stories of people who made mistakes and the consequences they faced so that they can learn from others' mistakes. Also point them to success stories around them and show them good examples as parents. Actions they say, speak louder than words.

Make use of every opportunity to drive home a lesson. Tell them stories about your youthful days so that they can know you were practically once like they are. This helps children to repose trust in their parents. They believe their parents can understand their feelings and be able to help them out.

Apart from answering your children's questions, also ask them questions. Poke into their lives. Know their friends and how they are getting along in relationships. Sometimes, intrude into their privacy and be ready for surprises.

Discipline in love. Even when children make mistakes, still be there for them as parents. Parents should never give up on a child. A child that is rejected today could be the corner stone of the family tomorrow.

In conclusion, before children start having the urges and seeing the changes in their bodies, link them to God. Lay a solid foundation of a relationship with God for your children. Once they are hooked on God, the guidance becomes easier. God will always be there for them even when their parents are not around. It's very exciting to see children follow God.

"Train up a child in the way he should go: and when he is old, he will not depart from it" (Prov. 22:6)

May the good lord help us all to fulfil our roles as parents in the lives of our children (Amen).

References

1. Wikipedia, the free encyclopedia, "Virginity" (en.wikipedia.org).

2. Issues: Berkely Medical Journal, fall 1998 Edition (Restoring Virginity).

3. 20 Questions About Virginity: Scarleteen Interviews Hanne Blank

4. Issues: Beakly Medial Journal, fall 1990 Edition (Restoring Virginity).

5. Nemours foundation, "Sexually Transmitted diseases (STDs)" Reviewed by Larissa Hirch, MD

6. Dr James Dobson, "Complete Marriage and Family Home Reference Guide" Tyndale House Publishers, Inc (Pg 161)

7. The National Women's Health Information Center, U.S Department of Health and Human Services, Office of Women's Health, "Sexually Transmitted Diseases: Overview"

8. Ditto

9. Dr James Dobson, "Complete Marriage and Family Home Reference Guide" Tyndale House Publishers, Inc (Pg 162)

10. Ditto (Pg 161)

11. A O Osoba, "Sexually transmitted diseases in tropical Africa. A review of the present situation.", British Journal Of Venereal Diseases.

12. Coplan P, Okonofua F, Temin M, Renne E, Heggenhougen K, Kaufman J; International Conference on AIDS. Int Conf AIDS. 1998; 12: 640 (abstract no. 33239).

13. Merck Research Labs, West Point, PA 19486-0004, USA. Courtesy of: U.S. National Library Of Medicine.

14. The Communication Initiative Network10. American Social Health Associations, Inc, "Chlamydia" (ashastd.org)

15. The National Women's Health Information Center, U.S Department of Health and Human Services, Office of Women's Health, "Genital herpes"

16. Ditto

17. Ditto

18. Wikipedia, the free encyclopedia, "Gonorrhea" (en.wikipedia.org)

19. Emedicine Health, "Gonorrhea" (emedicinehealth.com)

20. Teenshealth, "Gonorrhea" (kidshealth.org)

21. American Social Health Associations, Inc, "Hepatitis" (ashastd.org)

22. Ditto

23. Wikipedia, the free encyclopedia, "Hepatitis" (en.wikipedia.org)

24. The National Women's Health Information Center, U.S Department of Health and Human Services, Office of Women's Health, "Sexually Transmitted Diseases: Overview"

25. Wikipedia, the free encyclopedia, "HIV/AIDS", (en.wikipedia.org)

26. Mayo Clinic, "HIV/AIDS", (Mayoclinic.com)

27. Wikipedia, the free encyclopedia, "HIV/AIDS", (en.wikipedia.org)

28. Ditto.

29. American Social Health Associations, Inc, "Pubic Lice" (ashastd.org)

30. Wikipedia, the free encyclopedia, "Syphilis", (en.wikipedia.org)

31. Emedicine Health, "Syphilis" (emedicinehealth.com)

32. The National Women's Health Information Center, U.S Department of Health and Human Services, Office of Women's Health, "Sexually Transmitted Diseases: Overview"

33. Wikipedia, the free encyclopedia, "Syphilis", (en.wikipedia.org)

34. Wikipedia, the free encyclopedia, "Trichomoniasis", (en.wikipedia.org)

35. Division of STD Prevention. Prevention of genital HPV infection and sequelae: Report of an external consultants' meeting. Atlanta, GA: Centers for Disease Control and Prevention, 1999.

36. National Cancer Institute, U.S. National Institute Of Health, "Human Papillomavirus (HPV)", (cancer.gov)

37. Parkin DM. The global health burden of infection-associated cancers in the year 2002. International Journal of Cancer 2006; 118:3030-3044.

38. National Cancer Institute, U.S. National Institute Of Health, "Human Papillomavirus (HPV)", (cancer.gov)

39. Wikipedia, the free encyclopedia, "Genital Warts", (en.wikipedia.org)

40. Emedicine Health, "Genital Warts" (emedicinehealth.com)

41. Wikipedia, the free encyclopedia, "Genital Warts", (en.wikipedia.org)

42. Ditto

43. American Social Health Associations, Inc, "Pelvic Inflammatory Disease (PID)" (ashastd.org)

44. Women's Health, London, "Pelvic Inflammatory Disease", (womenshealthlondon.org uk).

45. Ditto.

46. American Social Health Associations, Inc, "Pelvic Inflammatory Disease (PID)" (ashastd.org)

47. Ditto.

48. Wikipedia, the free encyclopedia, "Pelvic Inflammatory Disease (PID)", (en.wikipedia.org)

49. The National Women's Health Information Center, U.S Department of Health and Human Services, Office of Women's Health, "Sexually Transmitted Diseases: Overview"

50. Ditto

51. Dr James Dobson, "Complete Marriage and Family Home Reference Guide", Tyndale House Publishers, Inc (Pg 161)

52. Ditto (Pg162-163)

53. Christian Answers Network: "Why should I save sex for marriage?"PO Box 200 Gilbert AZ 85299 (christiananswers.net)

54. Christian Answers Network: "What if it's too late? What if I've already forfeited my sexual purity?" PO Box 200 Gilbert AZ 85299 (christiananswers.net)

55. Derek J. Wojcieth, "Question and Answer on Premarital Sex". 1995.

56. James Dobson, 'In defense of a little virginity', Focus on The Family. 1992

57. Theresa Grenshaw, from remarks made at the National conference on HIV, Washington DC, Nov. 15-18,1991.

58. Rush Limbaugh, "The Way Things Ought to Be" Pocket Books, New York. 1992.

59. Questions and answers on 'Fornication' by Layhands.com

60. Questions and answers on 'Fornication' by Layhands.com

61. Issues: Beakly Medial Journal, fall 1990 Edition (Restoring Virginity).

62. The National Women's Health Information Center, U.S Department of Health and Human Services, Office of Women's Health, "Sexual Assault".

63. Ditto

Contact:

Remi Oluyale
www.remioluyale.com

Email: info@remioluyale.com
Tel: +234 802 305 9599
Whatsapp: +2348023059599
Twitter: @remioluyale
Https://www.facebook.com/oluremi.oluyale

www.amazon.com/author/remioluyale